Start Po and its Lighthouse

History, Map and Guide

by

Roger Barrett

ORCHARD PUBLICATIONS
2 Orchard Close, Chudleigh, Devon TQ13 QLR
Telephone: (01626) 852714

Copyright © 2006
Roger Barrett

All rights reserved. No part of this publication may be reproduced, stored in a retrieval system, or transmitted in any form or by any means, without the prior permission of the copyright holder.

ISBN 1 898964 74 2

Printed by
Hedgerow Print, Crediton, Devon EX 17 1ES

ACKNOWLEDGEMENTS

A special thank you to all those who helped during my research for this book: Sir Geoffrey and Lady Newman, the present 'custodians of the light'; Colin Wortley, former District Maintenance Manager and Officer in Charge of the Trinity House Depot, Penzance; Phil Griffiths, Peter Kingston and Gordon Partridge, the last Trinity House 'keepers of the light'; Emma Skingley, Craig Martel and Frank Celano, all formerly of Trinity House; Cliff Cordrey, Trinity House; Kendall McDonald, shipwreck historian; Henry Alexander, author of *The Life and Death of the Liverpool Barque Dryad*; Nick Ansell of Start Farm; Jonathan Ansell, Jim Trout and Nick Heath, local residents; Dr John Merefield and Gordon Waterhouse, natural historians; Gerry Douglas-Sherwood of the Association of Lighthouse Keepers; Margaret Lorenz, Cookworthy Museum, Kingsbridge; Tony Rouse, West Country Studies Library, Exeter; Claire Pawley and Tim Stanger, local photographers; Bob Eaglesfield and Richard Webb for their editorial advice and last but not least, my fellow tour guides at the Lighthouse. The help given by all those who supplied illustrations is also gratefully acknowledged. Every effort has been made to trace copyright holders and the author and publisher apologise if any have been inadvertently omitted.

CONTENTS

Maps

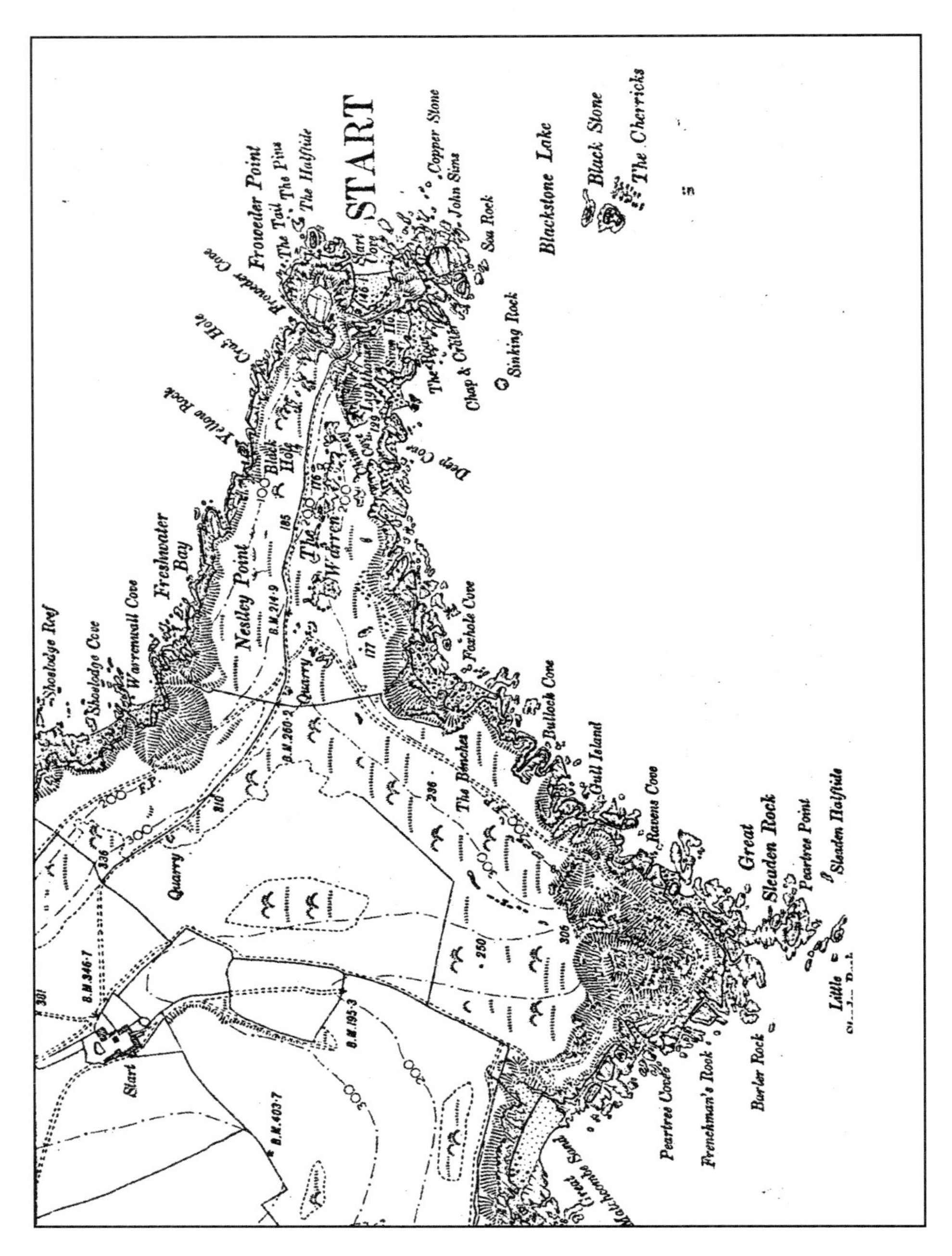

Extract from the 1886 Ordnance Survey Map showing Start and Peartree Points. (Ordnance Survey)

START POINT LIGHTHOUSE

Location: Stokenham Parish, South Devon
Grid reference: SX829371
Latitude: 50°13.344' N. Longitude: 003°38.539' W.
Light character: Group of three white flashes. Period: 10 seconds
Elevation of focal plane above MHWS: 62 metres (203ft)
Luminous range in sea miles: 25
Fixed red light over Skerries Bank, range in sea miles:12
Fog horn: 1 blast every 60 seconds
Height of tower: 28 metres (92ft)
First lit: 1836. Electrified: 1959. Automated: 1993.

1. THE SEA BE FAIR WICKED 'ERE

Start Point, one of the most exposed peninsulas on the English coast. (Frances Griffith, Devon County Council)

Sloping abruptly on either side, the jagged crest of Start Point runs for almost a mile into the sea. At its tip the chalk-white Lighthouse has stood for 170 years, its bright light guiding and comforting ships and their crews as they make their passage up and down the English Channel. Exposed to the brunt of the weather, the rugged peninsula, long known to mariners as *the Start*, can be a wild, elemental place where unyielding rock meets blasting wind and surging sea. When calm, the Start presents a less daunting aspect, with the bold white tower standing serenely against the deep turquoise sea and azure sky.

Projecting into the Channel in an east-facing direction, the Start is flanked to the north and east by the long, gentle sweep of Start Bay, with Torbay and the larger Lyme Bay extending to Portland Bill beyond. Turning the corner, to the south and west, where the prevailing winds and the long Atlantic swells give the

Start Point. (Trinty House)

waves greater force, the coastline takes on a more rugged character. Sailors like to claim that it was this change in the nature of the coast that gave the Start its name: the actual *start* of true deep-sea, blue-water sailing for those venturing west into the Atlantic and beyond. In fact the name is derived from the Anglo-Saxon word *Steort* meaning 'tail', as in the red-tailed bird, the Redstart.

The Anglo-Saxons probably had something more frightful in mind than a small bird when they named the Start, for its impressive ridge of highly metamorphosed schist rock, formed over 350 million years ago, has given rise to many metaphorical allusions to fearsome animals or monsters over the centuries, to the extent that the chart might well have read 'Here be Dragons'. Colourful examples include 'the Start with its long tongue of rock, a warted and horrent tongue like that of some primeval dragon,'…'the razor-backed ridge of demoniacal-looking humps of ironhard rock like the vertebrae of a crocodile's back', and 'the armoured back of a Stegosaurus'. Even the normally staid Admiralty Channel Pilot refers to the ridge's 'rugged cock's-comb appearance'.

Mariners have always enjoyed something of a love-hate relationship with the Start. The headland 'brought shipping, trading with London or the ports of North-West Europe, close to the coast (and) it has provided many a ship inward bound from the Atlantic Ocean with perhaps the first positive position after several days of uncertainty because of overcast skies in the Western Approaches'. [1]

But, although the Start has always been a welcome landfall and waymark for mariners, it is also notoriously hazardous, for as many ships have been wrecked on the reefs and shoals around the Point, as on any comparable headland in the British Isles. As far back as 1652, Thomas Fuller was warning of the dangers lying off the Start: 'It is more than suspicious that many hundreds have here had

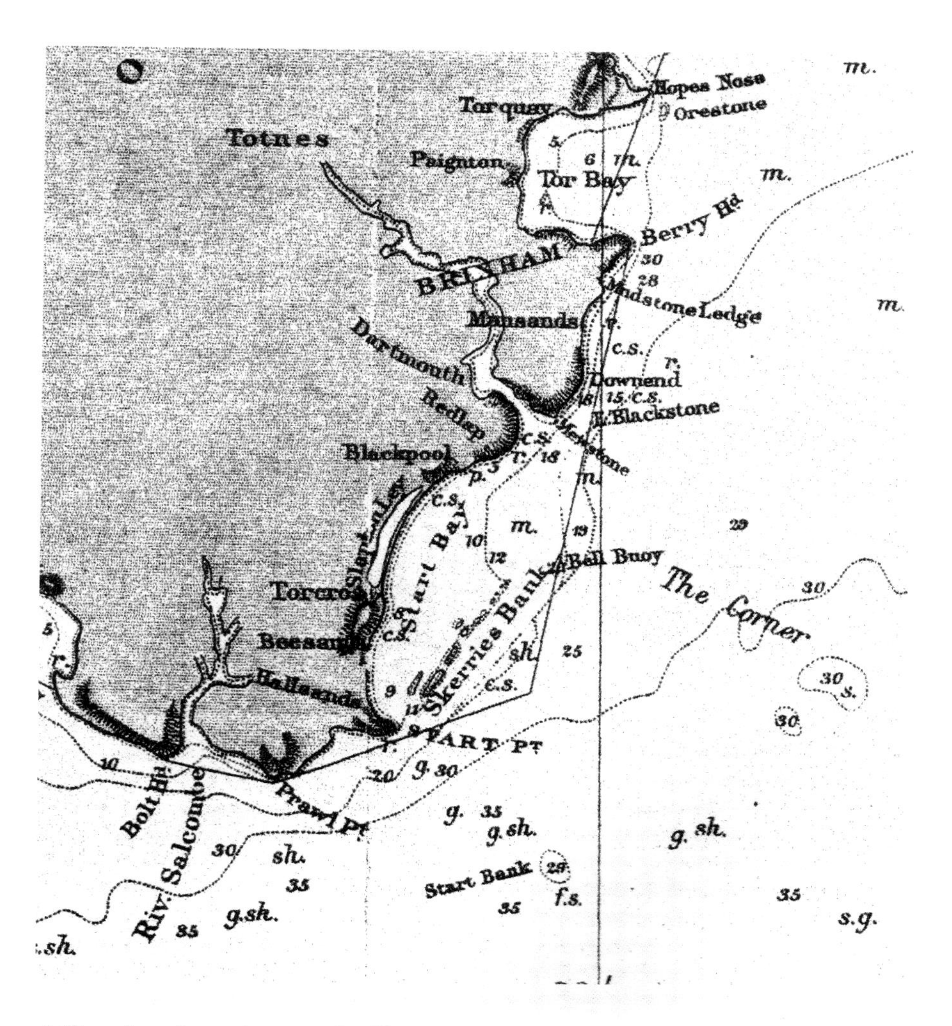

A Victorian chart showing the Skerries Bank. (Devon Sea Fisheries Committee)

there silent deaths, never landing to relate the cause of their destruction. Let all ships thereby be fore-armed because forewarned thereof, seeing these rocks can no otherwise be resisted than by avoiding'. [2]

The rocks which can only be 'resisted by avoiding' are the Black Stone, the Cherricks and to the west, the Great and Little Sleaden Rocks. Together they extend for a quarter of a mile to the south of the Point. They are not the only hazards. In Start Bay, the Skerries Bank, the only major offshore shoal in the West Country, extends over four miles to the north-east, and has a depth of only 6ft (2m) at the lowest tide. Tidal streams sweep south along the shore of Start Bay for eight hours out of twelve and spill through the narrow passage between the Skerries and the Start.

This gives rise to the Start Tidal Race, an often turbulent maelstrom of big seas and heavy over-falls, which sets for nearly a mile to southward of the Point. Even on a calm day the sea is disturbed with breaking white-crested waves caused by the strong eddies.

In the days when sailing ships fixed their position by hugging the coast, masters of vessels coming up-channel, would, all too often, alter course to the north-east towards the next headlands at Downend and Berry Head. The result was often a watery grave on or near the Skerries. Sharing that graveyard are the numerous ships that have been driven by an easterly or south-easterly gale onto the Skerries Bank, or onto the lee shore, between Start and Slapton. The reefs off Start could also be a death-trap for any ship caught without sufficient sea-room in a southerly gale.

In 1935 Raymond Cattell, after being warned by a Beesands fisherman that 'the zee be vair wicked yeer', sailed around the Start in his small boat, *Sandpiper*: 'For all sailors in tiny craft the rounding of the Start is an experience in itself. For it is the haunt of a fierce tidal race, which in rough weather spreads a dread regiment of enormous white horses two or three miles out to sea. Even in the calmest weather the surface of the sea is twisted and tortured as by a far-flung whirlpool and from which the maddest whisperings and groanings rise into the still air. Sailors swear that the spirits of drowned seaman meet here'.[3]

The turbulent waters of the Start Tidal Race. (Nick Heath)

2. EARLY HISTORY

A rather fanciful depiction of the defeat of the Spanish Armada off Start Point in 1588. (Devon County Council)

Saints and Sinners

It is possible that a light to guide seafarers and warn them of the perils off Start, shone here as far back as the Middle Ages. Most of the early maritime lights, such as the one established on St Michael's Mount, in Cornwall, during the fourteenth century, were of ecclesiastical origin and were often 'attached to votive chapels set up by some pious or grateful mariner'. A chapel dedicated to St Mary is known to have existed at, or near, Start in 1506, for on the 25th February of that year an 'indulgence of forty days (was) granted to all parishioners assisting in the repair of the chapel of the Blessed Mary of Stert in the parish of Stokinham'.[1] However, in 1540 the chapel was referred to as 'the chapel of St Mary of Hallsands'[2] and so it is possible that the chapel was erected there.

If the chapel was sited on Start Point, then its remains may still have existed in 1793, for Richard Polwhele, in his History of Devonshire published in that year, made the rather bizarre claim that the columns of a temple to the Syrian love and war goddess, Astarte, also known as Astoreth, were then to be seen on Start Point.[3]

None of the medieval chapel lights in South Devon survived the Reformation in the sixteenth century. Indeed in the latter part of that century a warning of a less friendly kind greeted mariners as they sailed past the Point. A gallows was erected here and from this was hung a grim reminder that acts of piracy would be met with the severest retribution. Stokenham Parish Register records that 'a pirate of the sea was hanged in chains upon Stert on the 28th day of September, in the year of our Lord 1581. His name was Henry Muge'.

Francis Drake's Guiding Light: The Great Armada of 1588

Seven years later another form of warning was to be seen above Start Point, the Armada Beacon on Beacon Hill (Beacon Hill is the name of a field to the north-east of the BBC transmitter site and the beacon is believed to have been sited near the top of the cliff above Start Bay).[4]

King Philip of Spain's Great Armada of 1588 was first sighted off the Lizard at dawn on 30 July. Fire beacons immediately flashed their warning along the coast. In the South Hams the beacon light passed in a chain through Thurlestone, Malborough, South Pool, Chivelstone, to the watchmen at Beacon Hill, above Start Bay. Their flames were then passed to Dartmouth and on to London via Dittisham and Torbay.

In the fading light of the following evening, the local people gathered on Start Point witnessed a spectacle of unsurpassed magnitude as 'the greatest navy that ever swam the sea' sailed by in slow procession. One hundred and twenty-five Spanish galleons and galleasses were to be seen spread over seven miles of sea in a mighty crescent formation. The English fleet, commanded by Lord Howard, was two miles astern and by the time it reached Start Point it was nearly dark.[5]

Earlier that evening Howard had called a council-of-war aboard his flagship, *Ark Royal*, and granted Sir Francis Drake the honour of leading the pursuit. Drake was ordered to show, at the stern of his *Revenge,* a guiding light for the 'blacked-out' fleet to follow. The watchers on Start Point may have seen that light, but not for long, for after clearing the Point, Drake extinguished it, an action which was to cause Martin Frobisher, one of the other great 'sea dogs' of the day, to call Drake a coward and a cheat and to threaten that he would 'spend the best blood in Drake's belly'.

Drake's failing light caused consternation in the English fleet. Most captains shortened sail. A few, including Howard, held their course and at dawn found themselves, without support, within the crescent formation of the Spanish fleet. When Drake finally rejoined the fleet halfway across Lyme Bay, it was with the news that he had come across the *Nuestra Senora del Rosario,* the crippled

Great Mattiscombe Sand and Lannacombe Bay with Prawle Point beyond. (Author)

flagship of Don Pedro de Valdes and had captured it, having first doused his stern light to avoid confusing the fleet. Few of his fellow captains doubted that Drake, ever the opportunist, had slipped off in the night in search of this rich prize.[6]

Warreners and Farmers

Start Point was once part of the large Manor of Stokenham. During the Middle Ages the area of coastal heathland beyond Start Gate, known as South Moor, was progressively enclosed and farmed and by 1309 an outlying farm, Start Farm, had been established in the 'waste'. An Inquest held in that year, into the lands of the manor of *Stoke in Hamme,* stated that 'there are at Le Stert, belonging to this manor, 60 acres of arable, 2½ acres of meadow and 200 acres of rough pasture and a water-mill'.[7] The land was demesne land—that is land retained by the lord of the manor in his personal possession.

Near the end of the Start Point peninsula a dry-stone wall, still in existence today, was built across the headland to seal off an area of forty five acres known as the Warren.[8] Here rabbits were caught by the warrener, with ferrets and nets, to provide a regular supply of fresh meat for the lord's table. When the demesne

An engraving of Start Point by the Leighton Brothers, 1880. (Devon County Council)

lands were sold in 1585 the warren was no longer required, but the rabbits would have remained in abundance and the likelihood is that rabbit stew regularly graced the lightkeepers' table from 1836 onwards.

Private Lights

The year 1836 was notable, not only for the fact that it was in that year Start Point Lighthouse was first lit, but it was also the year in which the Corporation of Trinity House took over responsibility for all lighthouses in England, Wales, the Channel Islands and Gibraltar. Prior to 1836 most lighthouses were built and operated commercially by private owners who were able to levy tolls on passing ships. Two early attempts to establish a private light on Start Point, by Jacob Moore in 1542 and by Sir John Coryton in 1675, failed however, for fear that as an aid to navigators, such a light would assist the King's enemies.[9]

Wreckers and Smugglers

Meanwhile, the rocks and shoals around Start Point continued to claim their victims, the lack of action reflecting a general indifference to those who lost their lives at sea. Many believed that it was the will of God when shipwreck victims drowned and, for those living in poor coastal communities, survivors were often seen as a threat to their 'right' to plunder. Between 1236 and 1771 the law stated that if any man or beast escaped alive from a ship, then the ship was not a wreck — a powerful incentive for the local populace to ensure that no man or beast did indeed survive!

Whilst it is unlikely that ships were deliberately lured by guiding lights onto the rocks off Start by wreckers, the looting of wrecks was common practice. One often recounted story of the 1700s tells of the parson at East Portlemouth church who, when interrupted in his sermon with news of a wreck, informed his assembled flock that 'there's a ship ashore between Prawle and Pear Tree Point. Now steady lads, just one more prayer, and then we'll all start fair'. Rushing to Great Mattiscombe Sand, the parson and his congregation found a valuable Spanish galleon on the rocks.

Smugglers landing their contraband. Etching by J. A. Atkinson. (Alan Hay collection)

Local legend has it that the stranded crew shouted for a rope, but the one that was thrown was too short, and when the cry went up for 'more rope!', the hapless mariners were abandoned to their fate because 'dead men told no tales'. Great Mattiscombe Sand, which can be reached by a footpath from Start Point car park, was apparently long known as 'More Rope Bay'.

Whilst not all eighteenth century Devonshire parsons would have been such enthusiastic wreckers as the reverend gentleman of East Portlemouth, many would have been happy to dabble in that other important source of local income, smuggling: 'Five and twenty ponies, trotting through the dark, brandy for the parson, 'baccy for the Clerk'.

In the 1780s smuggling was being carried out on a large scale between Start and Prawle, and Richard Valentine, the Customs officer at Salcombe, reported that he had been threatened with having his brains blown out by the riders of not just five and twenty ponies, but a hundred, each armed with a brace of pistols, and waiting in readiness to bring smuggled goods ashore.[10]

He and his men had made considerable seizures along the coast between Start Point and East Prawle, but the smugglers had now become so violent that he needed the help of the horse troop stationed at Kingsbridge to deal with the problem. Whether the troopers turned out is not recorded, but at least Richard Valentine survived to the good age of seventy-five.

The north side of Start Point. The medieval rabbit warren extended from the middle ground in this photo to the tip of the headland. (Author)

3. THE THREAT FROM FRANCE 1793-1815

Admiralty Signal Station

When war broke out against Revolutionary France in 1793, the Channel coast was exposed to the threat of commerce raiding and invasion. To counter this, the Admiralty set up a series of 'early warning' signal stations in prominent coastal locations. Start Point signal station, established in 1795, had visual contact across Start Bay with Coleton ten miles NNE and with Hurter's Top at Prawle Point to the west.[1]

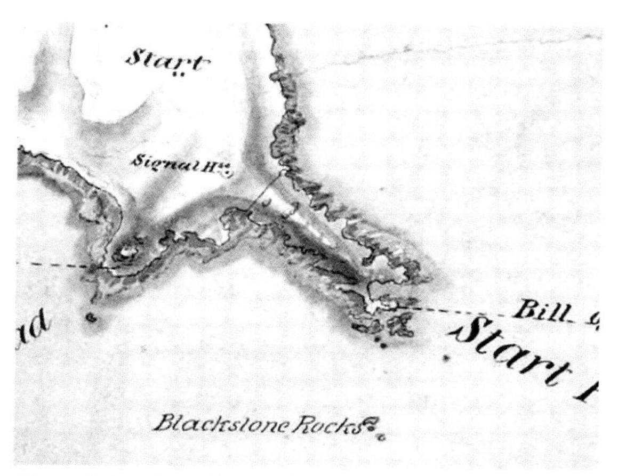

Site of the Start Point Signal Station as shown on James Walker's survey drawing of 1834. (Trinity House)

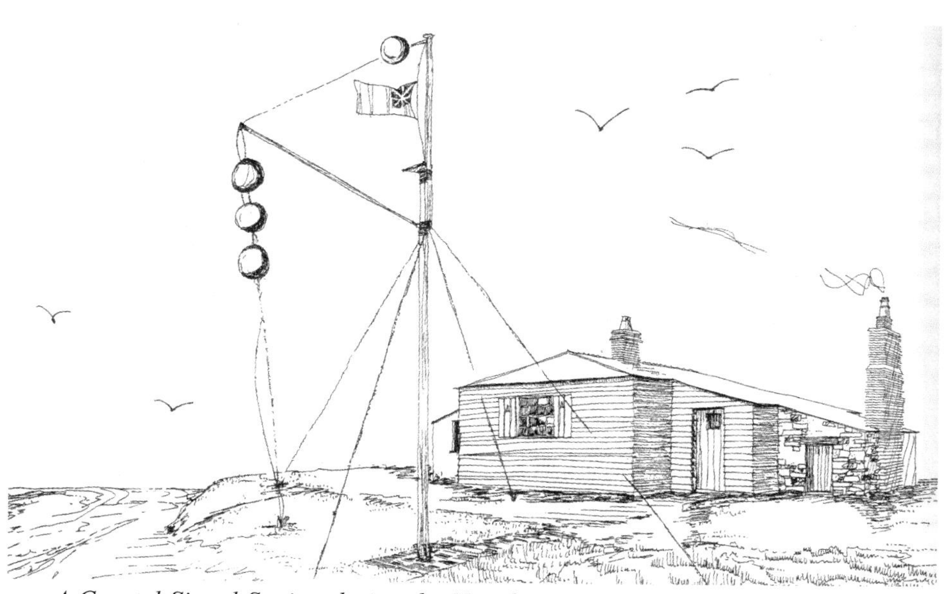

A Coastal Signal Station during the Napoleonic Wars. (John Goodwin)

The signal station was sited at the top of the 394 ft (120m) hill above Start and Peartree Points, in the eastern corner of the field called Colligo, (many years later the mast of a radar station was to be erected on the same spot). The station was commanded by a half-pay naval lieutenant, assisted by a midshipman and two men. They lived on site in a two-roomed hut.

During daylight hours, coded messages were sent by means of flags, as well as black canvas balls measuring over 3ft (1m) in diameter. A pennant flying on the mast, with three balls hung from the gaff, signified 'enemy landing to the westward'. The message would have included the number of the station—Start Point was number fifteen. For night signals, furze faggots or tar barrels were burnt. Suspicious coastal shipping was then investigated by fast naval sloops, after warnings had been passed along the chain to Maker Heights above Plymouth.

The station remained in operation, possibly as a semaphore station, after the defeat of Napoleon in 1815, in order to assist the revenue service in combating smuggling—still rife, no doubt, in Lannacombe Bay.[2] In 1816 the station was commanded by a Lieutenant Clayson. If he was in post at Start in August 1815, he would have witnessed one of the great events of the century, when the 'Great Ogre' himself sailed by.

'Boney' contemplates suicide off Start Point

Four weeks after his defeat at Waterloo on 18 June 1815, the Emperor Napoleon Bonaparte stepped aboard *HMS Bellerophon* (affectionately known as the *Billy Ruffian)* off Rochefort and offered his surrender to her captain, Captain Maitland. Maitland then sailed with his prisoner for England. After passing Start Point, the *Bellerophon* arrived at Brixham on 24 July. News of the arrival of the 'most famous person in the western world' leaked out and soon the harbour was full of boats crammed with curious sightseers. Two days later Maitland was ordered to sail for Plymouth and just before 8.00 am on the 26th the *Bellerophon* was off Start Point again, and heading west to pass Bolt Head, with Napoleon on deck observing the rocky coastline.

At Plymouth the ship was again besieged by sightseers, and on 3 August, the Government, having decided to transport Bonaparte on *HMS Northumberland* to his place of exile, St Helena, ordered Admiral Keith to put to sea with the *Bellerophon*, the 80-gun ship *Tonnant* and escorting frigates and await the arrival of *Northumberland* off Start Point.

Napoleon on board the Bellerophon. Oil painting by Sir William Quiller Orchardson, 1880. (Tate Gallery, London)

'For two days the ships waited off the coast between Start Point and Bolt Head. The grey sea under the louring, grey sky seemed to reflect the air of gloom which had settled over the passengers on the Bellerophon. Napoleon became increasingly depressed. He no longer appeared on deck but remained shut in his cabin...at one stage he talked about ending his life'. [3] On 8 August Napoleon and his followers transferred to *HMS Northumberland* and then 'vanished into exile over the horizon'.

4. BUILDING THE LIGHTHOUSE

James Walker 1781-1862. (Institute of Civil Engineers)

By the early 1830s, the dangers posed to shipping by the rocks and shoals off Start Point could no longer be ignored. The sharp rise in sea trade arising from the Industrial Revolution had been matched by a tragic increase in the number of ships lost off the coast of South Devon. The Admiralty applied for a light on Start in 1827[1] and, finally in 1833, three years before an Act of Parliament which effectively nationalised the provision of lighthouses, Trinity House instructed their consultant engineer, James Walker, to draw up plans for a new lighthouse at, or near, Start Point.

James Walker was born in Falkirk in 1781. He was appointed consultant engineer to Trinity House in 1825, a post he held right up until his death in 1862. During that time he designed twenty nine lighthouse towers, including such famous lights as Wolf Rock, Bishop Rock, Casquets and the Needles. He also built some notable bridges, including Westminster and Vauxhall Bridges in London. Walker's epitaph, on his Edinburgh tombstone, described him as 'upright, sincere and unostentatious in his life, unsparing of himself'. A man of slight build, he was said to be 'a strict disciplinarian and indefatigable in his attention to the works under his charge'.[2]

Painting of the Lighthouse by R. H. Froude, 1846. (Devon County Council)

The selection of the actual site for the new light was a matter of some debate. The Wardens' Committee of Trinity House had originally

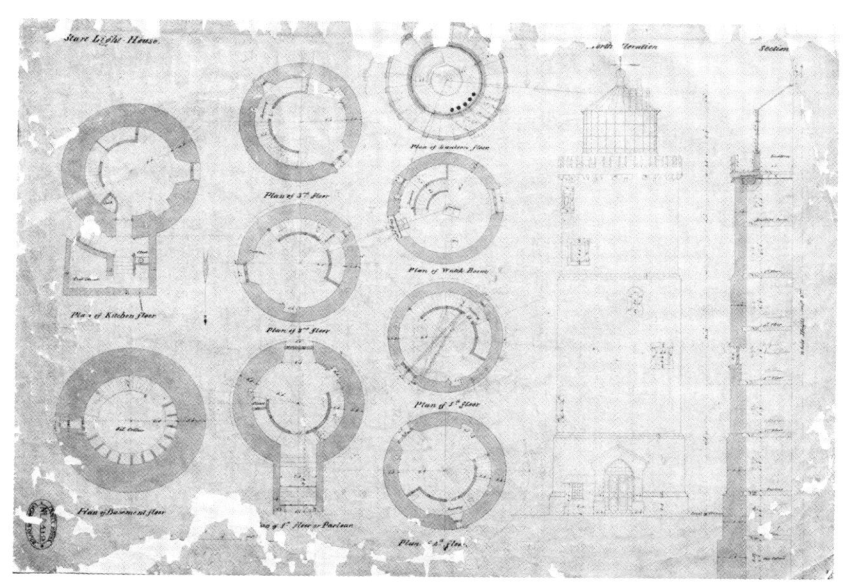

Plans, elevation and section of the nine floors of James Walker's lighthouse.

recommended Prawle Point, four miles to the west of Start, and was supported in this by the Plymouth Chamber of Commerce. However, in September 1833, the Elder Brethren directed that the lighthouse should be 'erected at Start Point on the cockscomb where it is of nearly the same elevation as the table land upon the Prawle'. The site was to be purchased from Edmund Bastard Esq., but it was not until 1849 that the land was formally conveyed to the Corporation at a price of £42.

One of Walker's drawings. (Trinity House)

In March 1834 Trinity House, having obtained Letters Patent authorising the collections of tolls from vessels passing the Point, approved James Walker's designs for a round tower 'constructed of the best quality stone, which the rocks at Start Point afford, faced with granite'.

The 67ft (20.5m) high stone tower was to be constructed with eighty courses of dressed granite, rising in three diminishing stages.

At its base the walls were to be 4ft 6ins (1.4m) thick, reducing to 2ft (0.6m) thick in the upper stage. Surmounting the stone tower, and rising above its battlemented parapet, Walker designed a 20ft (6m) high lantern, with rectangular glass panes, capped with a conical canopy. His design owed much to the 'gothic' style of architecture in vogue at the time.

In May 1834, Hugh McIntosh, having submitted the lowest tender of £2765, was selected as contractor for the building works. James Walker later described McIntosh as 'the principal contractor for public works in England'. He was born in Nairn, Scotland in 1768 and began his career as a 'navvy' on the Forth-Clyde Canal. He went on to become a prolific builder of canals, docks, railways and bridges and by 1834, he was said to have 'the reputation of being worth £1,000,000 of money'. He remained active until his death in 1840. [3]

Etching by E. Edwards, 1863. (Devon County Council)

Sarah Fox, writing about the Lighthouse in 1864 said that 'the name of the engineer that undertook the work was Abernethy, and that of the contractor was McIntosh, who, although blind, was an active inspector (so to speak) of the business in hand!'[4] McIntosh, had become blind after working on a canal in 1826. His twenty year old, resident engineer at Start Point, James Abernethy, described 'how McIntosh, by then a blind old man, inspected the works with the help of his agents...and kept tight control on site visits by asking detailed questions'. Abernethy, like Walker and McIntosh, was a Scot, and like Walker before him, was to rise in his profession to become President of the Institute of Civil Engineers. He was a prolific builder of harbours and docks, including Falmouth Pier and Graving Dock and Swansea South Docks.

'McIntosh organised a work force of forty men, who ranged from masons to labourers, quarrymen, carpenters, a blacksmith and ten stonecutters who would prepare all the masonry'. [5] The local stone—green schist—provided the rubble infill and was presumably obtained from the two quarries marked on the 1886 Ordnance Survey map (see map on page iv). The granite facing stones would have been brought in by boat, but their source is not known. One possibility is Colcerrow Quarry in Cornwall, which supplied the stone for the Plymouth Breakwater Lighthouse in 1841-44.

The Lighthouse on its cliff-top perch. (Trinty House)

A decision on the lights to be exhibited was not made until January 1835. The main optic was to be the first of its kind in the Trinity House service: 'a revolving light of the first order, similar to that of Corduan Lighthouse'. This was a reference to the dioptric apparatus invented by the Frenchman, Augustin Fresnel, and installed by him in 1823, in what is probably the world's most magnificent lighthouse, Corduan, near Bordeaux. Fresnel's optic comprised a central bull's eye lens, which focused the rays from the lamp, surrounded by concentric rings of prisms which refracted or bent any remaining light and drove it outwards in a single compact beam. A secondary fixed white light was also to be shown to mark the Skerries Bank.

Argand oil burners, invented by the Swiss scientist Aimé Argand in 1784, provided the light source in both cases. The Argand burner had a circular wick and a glass funnel to provide a good draught. The fuel was probably sperm-whale oil, but rape-seed oil (colza), herring oil and seal oil may also have been used, depending on the price.

An order for the new lights was placed with Messrs Cookson of Newcastle in February 1835, but four months later the firm admitted that they lacked the knowledge to fix the lenses and mirrors to the optic framework. So the Board turned to James Walker's counterpart in Scotland, Alan Stevenson, who had made an extensive study of the Fresnel system. Stevenson agreed to provide the framework and revolving machinery and help Cookson prepare and fit the lenses.

By February 1836, Stevenson had shipped the apparatus from Leith in the steam packet *Royal Victoria.* It weighed nearly four tons and, when it arrived, Walker was faced with the difficult task of getting it safely ashore at the landing place he had built on the east side of the cliff at Froweder Point (see map on page 29). An engraved stone dated 1835, and marking the high water level, still remains on the rock-cut steps. After being lifted by a crane from the boat the apparatus was then raised 112ft (34m) to the base of the tower, and then up the 92ft (28m) tower itself. Once there, it had to be placed carefully on the roller bearings in the pedestal base, so that it rotated smoothly when the clockwork mechanism was turned on.

On the evening of Friday, the 1st of July 1836, one year before Queen Victoria came to the throne, the Lighthouse was illuminated for the first time. It had taken two years to build and cost £5892. Below the lantern room were two service floors, four floors of living accommodation, the lowest of which was the keeper's parlour, and two basement levels: the upper, a kitchen with a coal store, the lower, an oil store. The kitchen, the four living room floors and the lower service room all had a fireplace with the chimney flues running through the thickness of the walls and up through the lantern canopy. The height of the light above sea level (measuring from the mean high water spring tide level to the centre of the lantern) was 203ft (62m) and its range was 21 miles (the range today is 25 miles).

The new light was an immediate boon for mariners, for a pilot going down-channel merely had to keep the light on his right to avoid running into Start Bay. In the three years from 1839 to 1841 the lighthouse provided Trinity House with an average profit of £555 a year in light dues.

Masters of homeward-bound ships, particularly those making passage up-channel from Ushant and the Bay of Biscay, would chart their course to make a landfall at the Start. The Lighthouse provided the waymark, whilst, between 1868 and 1956, the signal station at nearby Prawle (a Lloyd's station from 1882), offered the means of signalling safe arrival back in home waters to anxious owners.

The Lighthouse viewed from the east. (Author)

5. THE VICTORIAN AND EDWARDIAN LIGHTHOUSE

The Lighthouse at the beginning of the twentieth century. The flat roofed north dwelling was built in 1844, whilst the principal keeper's dwelling on the left was completed in 1882. The drum canopy above the lantern, in this photo, replaced the conical canopy with ball ventilator, seen in the next photo, in 1895. *(Cookworthy Museum)*

The ball ventilator above the lantern indicates that this photo was taken before 1895. A pony and trap waits outside the principal keeper's house while the lady poses for the camera. (Devon County Council)

The first principal keeper at Start was Thomas Watson, but he was succeeded a year later (in 1837) by a Somerset man, William Shoemack. Shoemack brought with him his wife and four children and had two further children whilst at Start. He was still in post at the time of the 1861 census. Until the late 1870s, the principal keeper had just one assistant (unlike offshore rock stations which, following the death of a keeper on the Smalls in 1801, were always manned by three keepers). At first the principal keeper (PK), his family, and the assistant keeper, a single man, all lived in the tower, but in 1844 a new house, the North Dwelling, was designed by James Walker and built by Weekes of Dodbrooke for £545. Shoemack preferred the tower, so his assistant, William Westmoreland, moved into the house.

James Walker also improved access to the Lighthouse by sea and land in 1844. He completed the landing place on the east side at Froweder Point, 'where the crane once stood', so as to allow boats to land at dead low water and built a new landing place in Start Cove to the south. At some stage between 1836 and

1844 Walker built a road down from Start Farm, for in 1844 he had plans approved for its repair, as well as for 'rebuilding the length of wall on the side of the road, and building buttresses where required'.

Meanwhile, the two keepers diligently kept the oil lights burning. Between them they had to light the two lamps ten minutes before sunset and watch them during the night, to ensure that the lights, and the machinery which worked the revolving optic, did not stop or get out of order. The Trinity House regulations required that, during the time the lights were lit, one keeper was to be constantly present in the lantern room and so the keepers took it in turns to 'watch the light, wind the clockwork and stare out to sea'. To fall asleep whilst on watch was the gravest offence a keeper could commit.

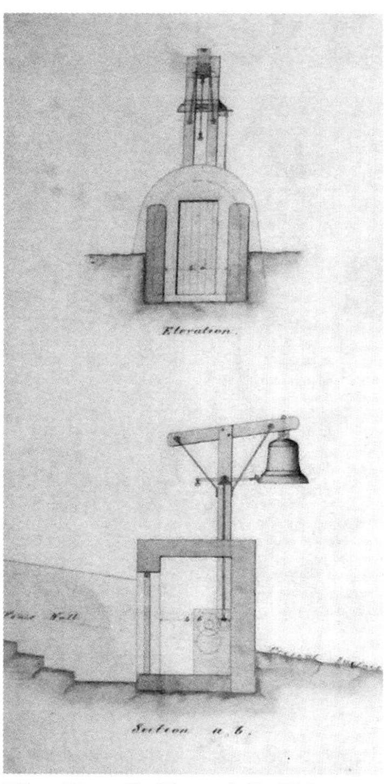

The Fog Bell and Bell-house erected in 1862. The bell was removed in 1876, but the building still remains. (Trinity House)

Sarah Fox, in her 1864 local guidebook, gave a fascinating account of a visit to the lighthouse, nearly thirty years after its completion: 'Visitors to the Start Lighthouse will be struck with the extreme neatness, as well as substantial quality. The apparatus and interior fittings are beautifully bright, and although it may be imagined that the two light-keepers must have much time on their hands, it does not appear to be so, the cleaning and trimming of the single Argand burner requiring the attention of both men for a large portion of every morning. Before we ascended the neat chalk-scored steps of the edifice to inspect the lantern, we were invited to have a look at the fog bell, erected in October of 1862. By means of a falling weight of about thirteen hundredweight, the huge clapper continues to strike the bell for about four and a half hours, without additional attention on the part of the attendants. The weight which gives motion to the machinery glides slowly down in a crevice of the rock'.

The small fog-bell house, with its barrel vaulted roof, still stands today, to the south east of the Lighthouse, perched inaccessibly on the eroded cliff. The 50ft

(15m) vertical crevice in the rock, down which the weights of the clockwork fell, was enclosed in masonry, and remains visible from Start Cove.

'While the light-keepers were finishing trimming the lamps, we waited in the neat parlour below, which was well supplied with good furniture and books; and heard, from the wife of one of the men, of the terrific storms, and great force of the wind at the exposed point of the Start. We expressed a fear that the children ran great risks on such occasions, but were assured that they had orders not to go outside when the wind was high and, she said, "they obey orders—everything must be kept in order here." Mounting the steps, we passed the neat dormitories.

'Immediately below the light-room is the apparatus for giving the slow revolution to the light, or rather to the system of glass prisms which reflect the fixed light. This beautiful wheel-work is kept in far greater order than any cathedral clock; every day it undergoes a thorough cleaning and oiling; the brasswork is finely polished, and the motion of the complicated train of wheels, was beautifully steady and even. The heavy weight which puts the whole in motion falls through a tube running through the centre of all the rooms to the base of the building. Ranged around this room are spare lamp-glasses, meteorological instruments, oil-cans, boxes for cloths, and various tools—each neatly labelled'.

'A short winding iron stair now leads us to the lamp-room. Here, glittering brass work and polished prisms of glass abound. The lamp is a series of Argands, one within another. There are four concentric burners and a beautiful arrangement for supplying and regulating the flow of oil. It is the ingenious arrangement of lenses—no polished metallic mirrors being used—which concentrates the light. In addition to this revolving light, there is a small fixed one, with a polished parabolic mirror, throwing a light only in the direction of and over a dangerous sand-bank (the Skerries)'.

Another visitor in the late nineteenth century, Walter White[2], described the rugged setting of the lighthouse: 'The buildings stand within a few yards of the verge of the cliff, the wall serving as a parapet, from which you look down on the jutting rocks beyond. You may descend by the narrow path, protected also by a low white wall. A rude steep stair, chipped in the rock, leads down still lower to a little cove and a narrow strip of beach at the foot of the cliffs. It is the landing place for the lighthouse keepers when they go fishing, but can only be used in calm weather'.

'The assistant-keeper spoke of the arrival of a visitor as a pleasure in the monotonous life of the establishment. Winter, he said, was a dreary time, not so

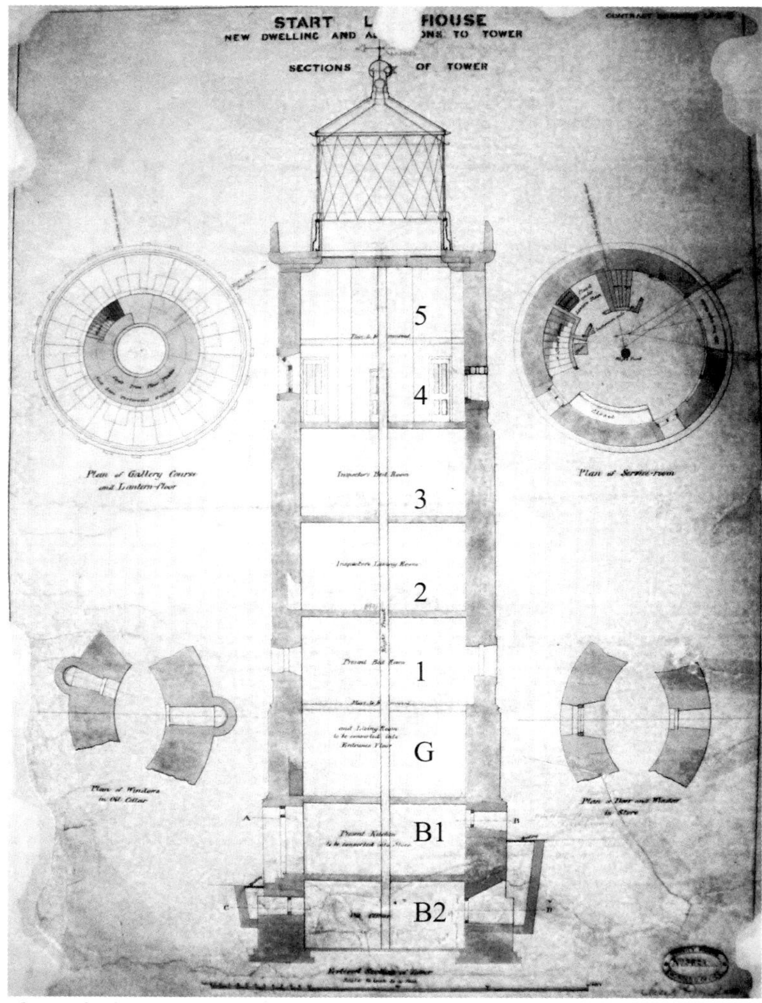

Section through the tower showing James Douglass's 1871 alterations, including the new lantern and the clockwork weight trunk down the centre. Key to floor levels:

B2 Oil cellar.
B1 Present kitchen to be converted to store.
G Living room converted to entrance floor.
1 Present bedroom. Floor to be removed.
2 Inspector's Living Room.
3 Inspector's Bedroom.
4 Service Room.
5 Floor to be removed.

(Trinity House)

much on account of cold, as of storms, fogs and wild weather generally. In easterly gales, the fury of the wind could often be such that to walk across the yard was impossible; they had to crawl under shelter of the wall and the spray flew from one side of the Point to the other. But indoors there was no lack of comfort, for the house was solidly built and conveniently fitted'.

By the end of 1871, the lighthouse machinery, so 'beautifully steady and even' when Sarah Fox visited in 1864, had become worn and uneven in its action and this prompted Trinity House to carry out a thorough overhaul. Plans for the new works were drawn up by their engineer-in-chief, James Douglass. Douglass, who lived for many years at Gramercy Tower in Dartmouth, was formerly an assistant to James Walker and succeeded the latter as Engineer-in-Chief to Trinity House in 1862. He went on to become one of the most celebrated of Victorian

A pre-1895 photo showing, to the right of the lighthouse tower, the South Dwelling built in 1873 and below it, the oil store and the round fog signal house built in 1876. Note the fog trumpet on the roof of the engine house. (Devon County Council)

lighthouse builders. Douglass's most notable achievement, for which he received a knighthood, was the Eddystone Lighthouse, which replaced Smeaton's Tower in 1882.

The works at Start included the erection of a new three storey house for the principal keeper, attached to the south side of the tower (the South Dwelling) and the removal of two of the stone floors in the tower (the first floor bedroom and the upper service room floor). New windows were inserted and some old ones closed. A stone store-room, for the paraffin oils to be used in the new light, was built to the south. Eighteen one-hundred-gallon oil tanks were installed on the slate bench that ran round the room (these were replaced in 1966 by a 1000 gallon tank). The building works were completed in 1873, by the masonry firm of Francis Chapman, from West Alvington, at a cost of £2800.

James Walker's lantern, with its rectangular glass panes, was replaced by James Douglass's revolutionary new Helical Lantern. This had curved diamond-shaped glazing and an integral ventilation system. 'Hit and miss' vents were fitted in the lantern's pedestal base to provide a constant flow of air over the inside of the glass, thus preventing condensation. The lantern's conical canopy also incorporated a ball ventilator. (The conical canopy was replaced in 1895 by the present drum ventilator).

The Fog Signal Engine House built in 1876. A party of boys wait at the entrance whilst their 'elders and betters' enjoy their picnic. (Devon County Council)

Inside the lantern a new optic, a dioptric light of the first order, weighing over three tons and with a petroleum burner, was installed by Chance Brothers of Birmingham, by then the world's leading producer of lighthouse optics. Chance Brothers also replaced the clockwork mechanism which rotated the heavy lenses, and introduced an ingenious arrangement whereby the fixed 'Skerries' light on the floor below, instead of having its own lamp, was lit by means of a reflector from the main lamp above.

On 20 December 1873, the *Kingsbridge Gazette* announced that 'the new petroleum light will be used this Friday evening at Start lighthouse. The illuminating power now used, it is considered, will render this the best light in the world, as all the latest improvements have been made available'. The fog bell, installed in October 1862, had long been considered unsatisfactory and was replaced in September 1876 by a powerful fog siren. This was installed in a circular fog signal house built by Chapmans to the south of the lighthouse. The new siren was 'sounded with air compressed by means of caloric engines of great power, which also rotates the siren disc. A sound of surpassing power is generated and the sound issues from the mouth of the cast iron trumpet in a condensed beam of great intensity. The siren gives three blasts—high, low, high—quickly every three minutes. In foggy weather the fog-siren is frequently heard at Salcombe'.[3]

Start Cove. Access to the beach was by means of steps cut into the cliff face on the right. (Cookworthy Museum)

The fog siren was of a type originally designed by Brown Brothers of New York for operation by steam pressure, but later adapted by James Douglass for use with compressed air. This was forced through a drum, fitted into the throat of the long cast-iron trumpet, in which a perforated disc spun at 2400 rpm against another fixed perforated disc. The trumpet was installed on the roof of the circular fog signal house.

Large quantities of coal would have been required to fuel the two fog signal engines, as well as for domestic cooking and heating, whilst the lighthouse lamp itself consumed 1750 gallons (8000 litres) of oil a year. Transporting all this fuel was a major undertaking. The nearest public road ended at Start Gate just above

The ruined village of Hallsands looking towards Start Point. The village was destroyed by a violent storm during the night of 26 January 1917. (Claire Pawley)

A pre-1895 postcard showing the well-tended vegetable plots, with the pigsties to the right and the original fog signal house to the left. (Assoc. of Lighthouse Keepers)

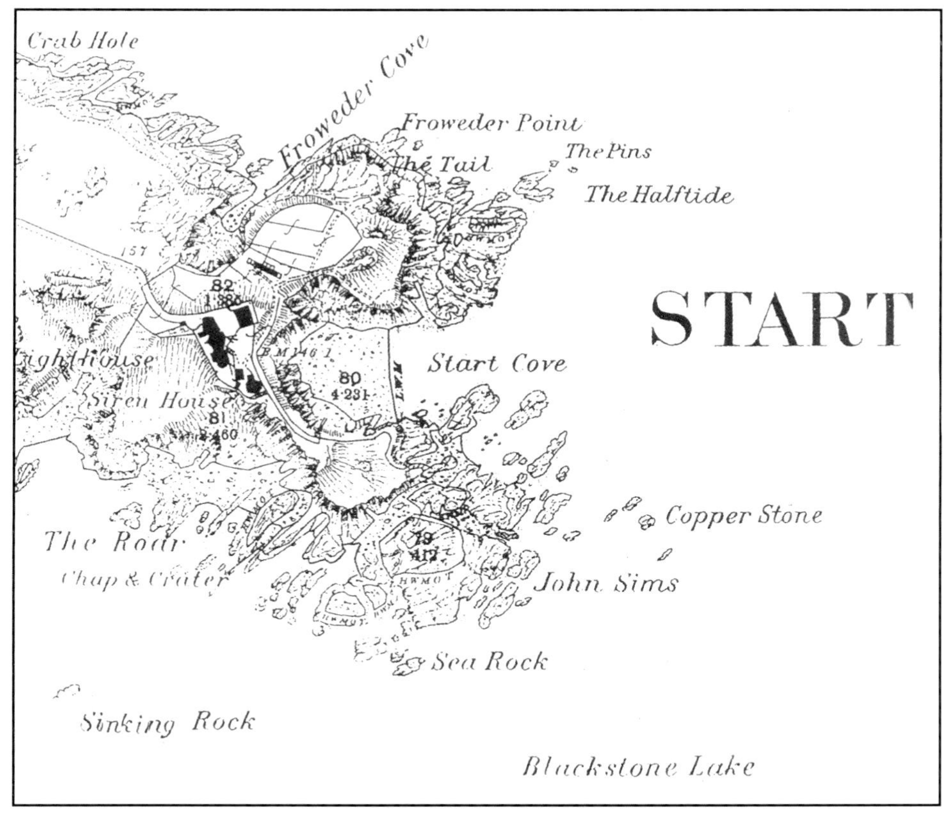

Extract from the 1886 Ordnance Survey Map. (Ordnance Survey)

Hollowcombe Head, one and a half miles away, and writing in 1884 James Fairweather confirmed that 'the only road from the Start is a high footway leading to Torcross northward along the cliffs'.[4] James Walker had constructed a private road down from Start Farm soon after the lighthouse was built, but wheeled traffic would have struggled on this, as well as on the narrow country lanes in the area, until their surfaces were macadamised in the 1920s. For at least eighty years after the Lighthouse was built, barrels of oil and most other bulk supplies were brought in by boat. Every June or July, a Trinity House vessel landed the annual supplies. Compared with the difficulties of supplying the offshore rock lighthouses, this would have been a relatively routine operation. Even so, it could only have been attempted in calm weather, and it would have been no easy task hauling the barrels of oil up the cliff. (It is not known if a cable hoist was used).

After the First World War, oil and coal were routinely brought in by means of horse and cart and later by motor lorry, after having been unloaded from a Trinity House supply vessel at Goodshelter, off South Pool Creek, or at East Portlemouth (both in the Salcombe Estuary).

The rugged coast between Start and Peartree Points. (Author)

In the days before 'proper' roads, Start Point was almost as isolated as an offshore site, and for many of the keepers, and more particularly for their wives and families, it must have felt like a 'punishment posting'. Offshore rock lighthouses had their own attraction for some keepers, but remote onshore sites, with families living in, were rarely popular. Only the occasional visitor and the itinerant packmen, who traded in cloth and fancy goods, relieved the monotony. In 1876 a shelter for a donkey and cart was built and in later years Trinity House provided first a pony and trap and then a motor taxi for a weekly shopping trip to Kingsbridge, ten miles away. Other than that, the nearest village was Hallsands, two miles to the north along the cliff path. Here there was a small shop, a bakery and the London Inn, well known for the 'white ale' brewed on the premises and where, in the 1890s, cider was a penny a pint, beer and ale 'thruppence'. (The inn was destroyed as a result of severe storms during the winter of 1903/4. Rebuilt, it was again destroyed, with the rest of the village, in January 1917).[5] In those days an inn was no place

A view of the peninsula from the Admiralty Channel Pilot. (The Admiralty)

for the keepers' wives and as they and their husbands were generally God-fearing folk, they were more likely to have sought comfort of a spiritual kind at the Hallsands Mission Room and from 1850, the Bible Christian Chapel, the ruins of which still lie perched above the cliff at Hallsands today.

The regular attendance of the keepers and their families at the Chapel prompted Trinity House to propose, in 1881, a donation of £10 and an annual contribution of £2 2s. (£2.10) for its upkeep. This met with an objection from the Board of Trade. It was this same government department that later resisted the compensation claims of Hallsands' villagers when their homes were destroyed in 1903/4 and 1917, almost certainly as a consequence of government authorised dredging in Start Bay.

The Keeper's Prayer Book. (Gordon Partridge)

As for the children, from 1876 when school attendance was made compulsory, there was a four mile walk to the little school at Huccombe, near Dunstone Cross. From 1900 the keepers at Start were able to send their children to board with friends or relatives in towns, in order to attend school, thanks to an allowance of £6 10s (£6.50) a year from Trinity House.

In 1880, the complexity of the new fog signal system prompted Trinity House to appoint a third keeper and by the following year the lighthouse community, which comprised just six souls in 1841, had grown to seventeen. To accommodate the growing population an additional acre and a half (0.6 hectares) of land was purchased from the then owner, A.J. Holdsworth Esq., for £75. On it a new house, now known as Beacon Cottage, was built for the head keeper in 1882, by the firm of Warrens for £1399. Gardens for all three families were laid out on the Tail, in the centre of which a fine range of outbuildings, comprising pigsties, with chicken coops above, wood and dustbin stores and a manure pit, were constructed.

Because of the remoteness of the station, the keepers and their families would have tried to be as self-sufficient as possible. The off-duty keepers fished and caught rabbits, whilst the wives and children tended the pigs and poultry. Vegetables

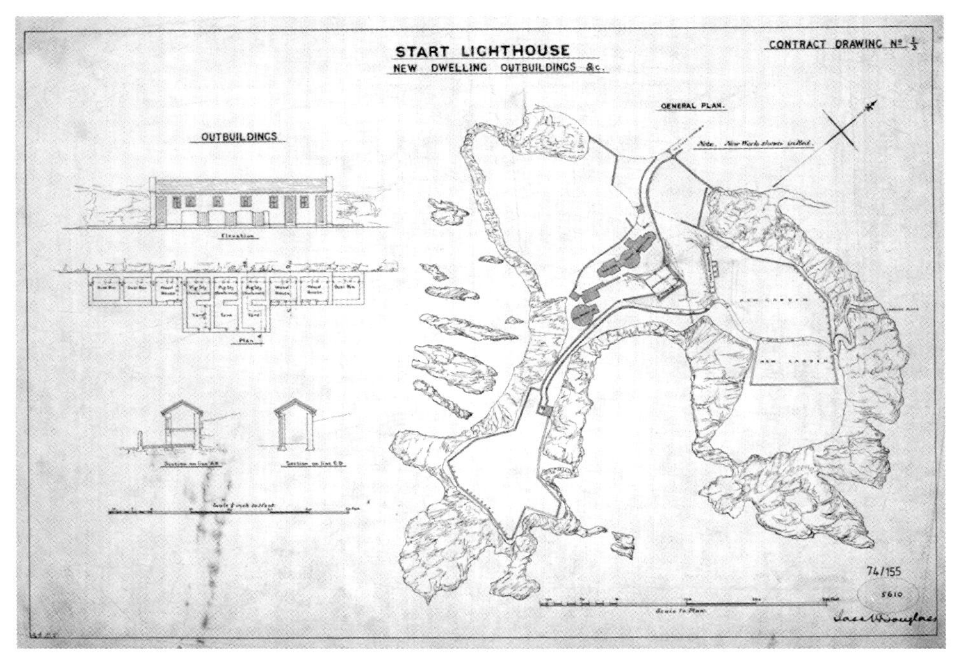

James Douglass's 1882 plan showing the site of the new principal keeper's house, the outbuildings, which included pigsties and chicken coops, and the garden plots. (Trinity House)

were grown on the terraced garden plots. Another valuable source of food was seagulls' eggs. Until recently there was a colony of over two hundred breeding pairs nesting each year on the slopes near the lighthouse and these were 'farmed' by the keepers' families who were careful to collect only one egg from each nest. Milk was brought down from Start Farm. Water came from the well-house to the north-west of the tower—the well, or rather the tank, being supplied by open channels from the slate-covered catchment area on the ground where the garages now stand. From the well-house the water, flavoured, no doubt, by salt spray, seagull droppings and other debris, was fed by pipes to ornate cast iron pumps in the scullery of each house.

It would be interesting to know how the members of this isolated community got on with one another. One imagines a strict 'pecking order' with the principal keeper's wife ruling the roost. This did not always apply, for 'at one English light, the assistant keeper's wife started a long and bitter fight with the principal's wife

The two interesting features in this post 1895 view are the slate covered water catchment area in the foreground and the twin bell-mouthed fog siren trumpets on the roof of the fog signal engine house. (Cookworthy Museum)

because one had a doorstep to her cottage and the other didn't!' Robert Louis Stevenson, a member of the great family of 'Lighthouse Stevensons' once observed, in relation to Scottish lightkeepers, that they 'usually pass their time by the pleasant human expedient of quarrelling and sometimes, I am assured, not one of the three is on speaking terms with any other. Their families are with them, living cheek by jowl. The children quarrel; Jockie hits Jimsie in the eye, and the mothers make haste to mingle in the dissention. Perhaps there is trouble about a broken dish; perhaps Mrs Assistant is more highly born than Mrs Principal and gives herself airs; and the men are drawn in'. But as Robert Louis' grandfather, Robert Stevenson, knowingly remarked 'the lightkeepers, agreeing ill, keep one another to their duty'. [6]

The keepers certainly had enough work to keep them at their duty. Oil had to be carried up to the service room, the wicks of the oil burners trimmed, the brasswork, optics and lantern glass regularly polished, the machinery oiled. The

A fine 1950's postcard view showing the line of the narrow approach road. (Aero Pictorial Ltd)

clockwork was wound up at regular intervals and the lamp lit before sunset and put out after sunrise. Passing vessels were logged and signalled to and regular weather reports maintained. In the fog signal house the port and starboard engines were lit and stoked up to maintain a pressure of 24lb psi in readiness for when Peartree Point to the west, or the white cottages at Beesands were obscured by fog during the day, or strong rays issued from the lantern at night. During the spring and summer months the tower, the buildings and the boundary walls were limewashed and the oil and water tanks cleaned.

In addition to a formal annual inspection, the District Superintendent and Trinity House 'top brass' regularly made unannounced visits, recording their findings in the Station Order Book. It is not difficult to imagine the frenzied activity on the part of the keepers and their families, as they rushed around to get everything neat and tidy, when a Trinity House yacht was seen approaching! Even more unexpected were the visits made by land after 'lighting up time'. The 'VIP' visitors generally found everything in good order, but on occasions standards slipped, with the principal keeper receiving a reprimand for 'not lighting up at the proper time', or for the fact that 'the lantern glass could not have been cleaned for days!'

Lighthouse stations were always hazardous places in which to live and work, not least because of all the combustible materials required to keep the light burning and the fog signal engines turning. Surprisingly, however, in the period from 1851 to the last days of permanent manning in 1993, the Station Order Book records only one serious accident. This occurred in 1880 when a supernumerary keeper, Mr Parsons, fell over the cliff. Fortunately, he was rescued and made a full recovery.

Between 1890 and 1897 inspections regularly revealed that the revolving apparatus for the main light was too slow. In 1897 the problem was finally rectified when mechanics from the Blackwall depot of Trinity House arrived to install new roller bearing wheels. These were set in a mercury flotation tray, a relatively new innovation which allowed the massive optic to rotate on a virtually friction free bed—so freely, in fact, that a child could revolve the light with a little finger.

Technological change continued apace into the twentieth century and in 1904 the Argand burner in the lighthouse lamp was replaced by a Matthews single mantle incandescent oil burner. This used vaporised paraffin, heated by a methylated spirit lamp. In addition to trebling the light intensity, the new burner reduced oil consumption by half. Also in 1904, the character of the light was changed to a one second flash every twenty seconds.

The south side of the peninsula. (Author)

6. FOR THOSE IN PERIL ON THE SEA

Samuel Popplestone of Start Farm, the first recipient of the Albert Medal. (Illustrated London News)

Over the centuries the seabed around Start Point has become the graveyard of numerous ships and shipwrecked mariners and in the nineteenth century even the presence of a powerful lighthouse failed to put an end to the loss of life.

In 1854, for example, three ships were lost in collisions off Start. On 29 April 1854, the *Favourite*, carrying German emigrants to Baltimore, was struck, in foul weather off the Point, by the American vessel *Hesper*. Captain Hoegman of the *Favourite* had been asleep in his bunk, but when he rushed on deck and saw that his ship was doomed he had only one thought in mind—his own preservation. With impressive alacrity he leapt across onto the bows of the *Hesper* and was quickly followed by his first officer and four of his crew. Captain Hoegman's remaining ten crew members and his 191 passengers were left to perish.

Five months later the Norwegian barque *Oceanus* was run down off Start and fatally holed by an unidentified schooner, which then backed away and refused to offer assistance. Fortunately, the Brixham lugger *Hero* was nearby and was able to bring off the master of the *Oceanus* and all but one of his crew.

Spirit of the Ocean 1866

The timely arrival of the aptly named *Hero,* in September 1854, would appear to mark a turning point in the chronicles of wreck and rescue off Start Point, for after that date the story, thankfully, becomes one of selfless courage and humanity, rather than callous indifference, towards those in peril on the sea. Nothing could exemplify this more than the bravery shown by Samuel Popplestone of Start Farm in rescuing survivors from the *Spirit of the Ocean* in 1866, a deed for which he was to be honoured by becoming the first recipient of the Albert Medal for gallantry (the forerunner of the George Cross).

In the South Transept of Stokenham Church is a stained glass memorial window dedicated to the twenty-eight men who lost their lives on 23 March 1866

Engraving from the Illustrated London News of 7 April 1866 showing the remains of the wreck of Spirit of the Ocean in Foxhole Cove (bottom left).

The same scene today. (Author)

when the *Spirit of the Ocean* was lost off Start Point. The 578 ton sailing barque was sailing down-channel under storm sails, on a voyage from London to Halifax, Nova Scotia, with a general cargo, when a southerly gale flung her towards the Start. Her captain, realising that she was at the mercy of the winds, deliberately drove her ashore towards Foxhole Cove, just west of the Point. Samuel Popplestone, the local farmer, had seen the ship standing into danger and sent one of his men to warn the coastguards at Hallsands. He then grabbed a rope and climbed down the cliff to Foxhole Cove.

Unfortunately, the vessel struck a reef about 100 yds (90m) from shore and within minutes had broken in two. Part of the stern floated into the cliff as Mr Popplestone lowered himself down to the beach and then waded across the slippery rocks to where four men could be seen clinging to floating debris. Two of them were able to get to shore unaided and were guided to the base of the cliff and the other two, one of whom was the mate, were hauled across after Popplestone made repeated attempts to cast his rope across the surging waves. In one of these attempts Mr Popplestone was washed off the rocks into the sea, but he managed to regain the shore. Too weak to climb the cliff, rescuer and rescued waited until a search party arrived to haul them up. The *Kingsbridge Gazette* in reporting his act of heroism, made the appropriate comment that 'only those who have seen the spot can realise the peril in which Mr Popplestone stood when engaged in his noble work'.

The Great Blizzard, March 1891

More wrecks were to follow and on one terrible night in 1891 as many as fifty-two seamen were drowned, or died from exposure, when four ships were dashed onto the rocks around the Point, victims of one the most violent storms ever recorded on the coast of South Devon: the Great Blizzard of 9-10 March 1891.[1] North-easterly winds, which reached up to hurricane force, exposed ships in Start Bay that night to the perils of the Skerries sandbank and to the lee shore between Start Point and Beesands, whilst driving snowstorms reduced visibility to a matter of yards.

The greatest loss of life was suffered by the 2177 ton, schooner-rigged steamer, *Marana* of Liverpool, which, with twenty-eight crew, was bound from London to Colombo, Ceylon (now Sri Lanka) with a cargo of railway sleepers. It was between five and six o'clock in the evening of 9 March 1891 when, with her engines still at full ahead, the *Marana* struck the Black Stone rocks just below the Point.

On the night of 9 March 1891, the 2177 ton steamer Marana of Liverpool struck the Black Stone rocks and broke in two. Only three of the twenty eight crew survived. (Devon County Council)

View from Start Point looking north across Start Bay to Hallsands and Beesands showing the approximate positions of the barque Dryad and the schooners Lunesdale and Lizzie Ellen, when they were driven ashore in the Great Blizzard of 9 March 1891. (Claire Pawley)

Mary Briggs, wife of assistant keeper David Briggs, was looking out of her window when she saw a steamer close to the Point. Seconds later she saw her strike the rocks, broad-side on. She then ran and gave the alarm to Mr Jones, the principal keeper, who immediately sent a messenger to the coastguards at Hallsands. Jones then saw the steamer break in two, the stern part sinking near the rocks, whilst the fore part washed away and sank a short distance to the west. The sea was dashing over the rocks with great fury and seeing nothing of the crew, he assumed that they had all been drowned. Mrs Briggs, however, was sure that she had seen two boats in the water before the steamer struck.

Mary Briggs was right: two boats were launched from the doomed ship. The first, with twenty-two of the crew on board, later capsized off Horseley Cove, to the west and was dashed onto the rocks there. Just five men managed to struggle ashore and of these, two, in their weakened state, died of exposure in the snow-covered fields below Prawle Coastguard Station. The second, smaller boat was launched with the Captain, three mates, the Chief Engineer and a steward aboard. It was never seen again.

Later that night another large ship, the 1035 ton, fully rigged barque *Dryad* of Liverpool, sailing from Shields to Valparaiso, Chile with a crew of twenty-one, struck the rocks just a few hundred yards to the north of the lighthouse. Mr Jones, the principal keeper, was standing in the yard a little after midnight, when he saw ship's lights right under the headland. He called the other keepers and together they struggled down the cliffs, but they found no sign of a ship. The Hallsands coastguards had also seen lights in the same position, so they fired off a rocket to warn the vessel of her danger, but then the lights disappeared. The coastguards strained their eyes in the blinding snow to scan the shore, but the effort was so painful they had to give up. No sign of the *Dryad* or any other vessel could be discovered.[2]

At daylight the next morning a coastguard, Mr Pollybank, was sent from Hallsands towards the Start, to see if there were any signs of a wreck. About 500 yards (460m) farther into the Bay from where the *Dryad* struck, he discovered a man lying on a low rock, known as John Hatherley's Nose (possibly named after John Hatherley, a keeper at Eddystone lighthouse in 1760), and immediately ran to the Lighthouse for assistance. David Briggs, Mary Briggs' husband, returned with Pollybank to the rock with ropes. After a failed attempt to throw a rope to the stranded man, Briggs then tied it to himself and swam out to the rock, but before he could reach him, a heavy sea came and washed the poor man away.

Hallsands Coastguard Station. (Cookworthy Museum)

S. S. Cookham stranded in Start Bay on 8 January 1893. The crew were taken off by Hallsands Coastguards. Although holed forward, the Cookham was refloated and towed to Dartmouth for repair. (Cookworthy Museum)

It was a busy night for the keepers, coastguards and local fishermen. Further up the coast, at about the time the *Marana* had struck, the 141 ton three-masted schooner *Lunesdale* went ashore at Hallsands. Her four man crew clung to the rigging but, by the time the local fishermen and coastguard reached her, only the master could be saved.

Later that evening, word came that the 73 ton schooner, *Lizzie Ellen* of Chester, was wrecked at the foot of a cliff, north of Hallsands. The fisherman lowered themselves down and got a line to the vessel, saving the mate and a seaman. The terrified cabin boy refused to leave however, and he and the master, who had remained behind in an attempt to persuade the lad to leave, drowned together as the vessel was dashed to pieces. The following morning eight bodies came ashore —four identified as from the *Dryad*. All eight were buried in Stokenham churchyard. Less than a month later further tragedy was to occur when the *Sunderland*, a 642 ton steam collier, was lost on the Start.

On 8 January 1893, Hallsands Coastguards rescued nineteen men and six boy cadets, by breeches buoy, from the *S.S. Cookham* which had stranded in thick fog on the rocks between Start Point and Hallsands. Five months later Trinity House gave the Post Office permission to lay an electrical cable to the Start and arrangements were subsequently made 'by means of which casualties at sea could be reported by telegraph from the lighthouse'.

Hallsands. (Author)

7. THE GREAT WAR AND ITS AFTERMATH

A modern submarine in Start Bay. The waters off Start Point were a favoured hunting ground for German U-Boats during the Great War. (Claire Pawley)

The Approach of War

In April 1913 the question of security at the lighthouse was exercising the collective minds of the Trinity House Board. The perceived threat however, was not the crisis in the Balkans or the growing arms race with Germany, but ladies wielding sticks and umbrellas!

The principal keeper at Start was directed 'that in order to prevent damage to the apparatus or gear by Militant Suffragettes, you will caution the Keepers at your station to exercise the greatest care when visitors are being shown round the station. Visitors should be requested to leave muffs, sticks, umbrellas, &c. in the base of the tower. The Keepers are to be given wider discretion as regards refusal to admit lady visitors'. [1]

A year later it was clear that German Dreadnoughts posed a greater threat than umbrellas. In the summer of 1914 the writer, Hilaire Belloc, was cruising in the *Nona* off Start Point: 'We had just rounded the Start at dawn. I watched, over the quarter, the Start Light flashing pale and white in the broadening day, and at last extinguished, and then it was that there passed me the vision I shall remember for ever: like ghosts, a procession of great forms, all in line, hastening eastward. It was the Fleet recalled. Then I knew that war would come'. [2]

The U-Boat Menace

When war did come to the coast of South Devon the dangers posed by German U-boats, preying on coastal shipping, were so great that the Lighthouse could only be lit when it was required to guide passing convoys. On these occasions orders would be received from the District Naval Officer to show the lights at half-power. The sea off Start Point was a favoured hunting ground for U-boats venturing into Channel waters and at least twenty-five British or allied merchant ships were sunk within sight of the Lighthouse.

HMS Formidable, the 15,000 ton Battleship sunk in Start Bay by a U-boat on New Years Day, 1915.

Also lost off Start was the 15,000 ton battleship *HMS Formidable,* one of the most powerful ships in the British Navy. At 3.00am on New Years Day, 1915, she was cruising with the Channel Fleet in line ahead off Start Point, when she was hit by torpedoes from the German submarine *UB-24.* She sank within forty-five minutes. Of the three boats that managed to get safely away, one, a pinnace, made for Lyme Regis with sixty survivors. However, nine of the men died of exposure. Able Seaman John Cowan was 'presumed dead' on arrival at Lyme and was laid to rest with the other bodies in the cellar of the Pilot Boat Inn. The landlord's dog, named Lassie, is said to have stayed beside him, nuzzling him and keeping his body warm with its fur. After half an hour Able

Survivors of the Formidable being taken aboard the Provident from their cutter. (The Sphere Magazine)

Seaman Cowan stirred and later made a full recovery. Lassie was hailed as a hero and awarded two medals. The story is believed to have inspired the 1938 novel *Lassie* by Eric Knight and the subsequent films.

Another of *Formidable's* boats, a cutter with seventy men aboard, was in danger of sinking 'since it had a hole in one side stopped only by a pair of sailor's underpants'. [3] The cutter had been drifting for about twelve hours, with the men suffering horribly from exposure, when it was spotted off Berry Head by the little Brixham smack, *Provident, BM291,* skippered by William Pillar. With great skill, in atrocious conditions, Pillar managed, after a long struggle, to get a line across. All the men were safely transferred and were later landed at Brixham where they were generously treated. William Pillar and his crew received a silver gallantry medal for saving life at sea. The following year, *Provident* was herself sunk in the channel by a U-Boat. A new *Provident, BM28,* was built in 1924 with a grant from the government in recognition of Pillar's rescue and is still to be seen sailing off Start Point. Of the 780 men on *Formidable*, 547 were lost.

Two German U-boat commanders, Ober-leutnants Bieber of *UB-31* and Stoter of *UB-35,* were particularly active in the waters around Start in 1917. *UB-31* accounted for eleven British steamers, whilst Stoter in *UB-35* sank four.[4] *UB-31's* largest victim was the 12,350 ton, P&O liner *Medina.* Built in 1910, she had been chartered as a royal yacht to take King George V and Queen Mary to the 1911 coronation durbar in Delhi. With the outbreak of war, the *Medina* was armed and in April 1917 was returning from India with Lord Carmichael, the retiring Governor of Madras and 410 other passengers and crew. At 6.30 pm on 28 April she was torpedoed by Bieber in *UB-31*, when she was three miles ENE of Start Point. All but six of the passengers and crew were safely loaded into boats, which were then towed to Dartmouth. The *Medina*

The S.S. Medina, sunk by a U-boat off Start on 28 April 1917.

sunk at 7.15pm in sixty metres of water, taking with her Lord Carmichael's priceless collection of antiques. In 1986-7 the salvage vessel *Holger Dane* recovered some of the items. These were auctioned at Sothebys in 1988.

The hospital ship *Asturias*, 'showing her lights and illuminated red cross, was torpedoed without warning', on 20 March 1917, by a U-boat five miles south of Start Point with the loss of forty-five lives, including a number of nurses.[5] The ship managed to run ashore at Starehole Bay, near the entrance of the Salcombe-Kingsbridge Estuary about eight miles to the north-west, where the forty-four wounded were taken ashore and cared for at Sharpitor, now Overbecks House.

On 8 September 1917 a British steamer, believed to be the 3400 ton *S.S. Newholm*, was the victim of a German mine-laying submarine one mile off Start Point. A local woman, twenty-one year old Ella Trout, who had been made homeless when the village of Hallsands was destroyed by the sea in January of that year, was fishing in a small boat when she saw the explosion. She immediately rowed over a mile, through treacherous cross-currents, towards the sinking vessel and pulled a 'half drowned' sailor from the sea. Eight other men were also rescued by a motor boat. For her courageous act, Ella was awarded the OBE. After the

Ella Trout OBE (left) with her sister Patience.

War, Ella, and her elder sister Patience, built Trout's Hotel above the ruined fishing village. Contrary to a local tradition that its construction was funded by a gift from the rescued sailor's grateful parents, the money in fact came from their own hard labour, and from the meagre compensation of £150 received for their lost homes. [6]

In response to the U-boat threat off the South Devon coast, anti-submarine patrols were carried out by airships from Mullion in Cornwall, but these met with little success and high losses. In July 1916 airship *C8* crashed off Start Point killing three members of the crew. The anti-submarine aircraft based at Prawle airfield, three miles to the west, fared little better. *RNAS Prawle*, which opened in April 1917, was the first airfield established in the South West of England for land planes. Six of its Sopwith biplanes were involved in accidents within three months of delivery, and when, in April 1918, it re-opened as *RAF Prawle*, the flights of DH6s and DH9s also suffered from a high rate of accidental loss. [7]

The U-boat war was not entirely one-sided, however. Between March and November 1917, four German U-boats were sunk off Start, all believed to be victims of anti-submarine mines. The Admiralty followed up these successes in December 1917 by posting, to the Lighthouse, three officers and seventeen marines from the Submarine Mining Service. The officers were quartered in the principal keeper's cottage and the men in the assistant keepers' dwellings and in the tower. They remained there until the end of the war. One entry in the Station Order Book refers to the naval party being engaged in observation mining. With this method anchored mines were connected by an electric cable to the observation post and were detonated by the observer whenever a hostile ship passed over. No successes are recorded, but the mines may have had a deterrent effect for only one allied ship fell victim to a U-boat off Start in 1918. This was the *Agnete*, a 1127 ton armed merchantman torpedoed by *UB-40*, two miles south of the Point on 24 April 1918, with the loss of twelve of her crew.

Between the Wars

In 1922 a still more powerful petroleum vapour lamp was fitted in the Lighthouse. This was the Hood 'auto form' incandescent burner which, by incorporating a small air pressure system, allowed the mantle to expand to twice its size and, as a result produce a much brighter light. Illuminating it involved first lighting the methylated spirits in the brass cup in order to vaporise the paraffin as it was injected. The hissing vapour would then be lit near the mantle with a long taper. With the clockwork mechanism already primed, the dog clutch would then be dropped, the brake let off and the lens would slowly begin to pick up speed. To keep it turning the keepers wound up the clock every twenty minutes throughout the night.

One of the two Gardner, three-cylinder, T4 engines in service at Start Point between 1928 and 1968. (Birmingham City Museum)

In 1928 the fog warning system, installed in 1876, was replaced with a new Diaphone twelve-inch fog siren. This had a loud melodious note, ending with a distinctive 'grunt'. The sound was produced when a slotted piston was forced upwards, by compressed air, in a cylinder with matching slots. Compared with the compact electric emitter unit currently in use, the equipment required to produce this sound was vast: two cast-iron conical resonators were positioned one above the other in a steel siren turret attached to the roof of a new 40ft (12m) high fog signal tower. The tower was constructed of reinforced concrete and housed large air receiving tanks. The adjacent engine room, in the circular 1876 building, housed the Reavell air compressors driven by two, three-cylinder Gardner T4 oil-fired engines, and two huge air storage receivers. Also in the engine room was a Lister diesel engine, coupled to a Higgs 10kW standby electric generator.

A view of the Lighthouse showing the radio beacon on the rocky ridge above. (Roy Westlake)

To the west of the engine room was a two-storey building with a watch house and radio room above the battery room. The watch house was manned when the fog siren was in operation. To the north was the oil store built in 1873 and, to the north-east, a reinforced concrete structure built in 1928 to house two, 4600 cubic feet water tanks for the water-cooled engines. This building, which is the only part of the fog siren complex still standing, had a flat roof to catch rain-water.

A wireless fog signal, in the form of a radio beacon, was also installed, with the beacon mast set up on the rocky ridge of the Point just above the Lighthouse. The call sign, originally GSM but SP from the 1950s, was given out in morse code every six minutes and provided the navigator, using direction-finding equipment, with a bearing from a fixed point. He could then fix his ship's position at the point where it was 'crossed' by the bearings from other stations in the 'Channel West' group, which included Penlee Point, the Lizard, the Casquets on the Channel Islands and two stations on the French coast. The beacon had a range of seventy nautical miles and continued to send out its signal on 298.8 kHz right up until April 1992.

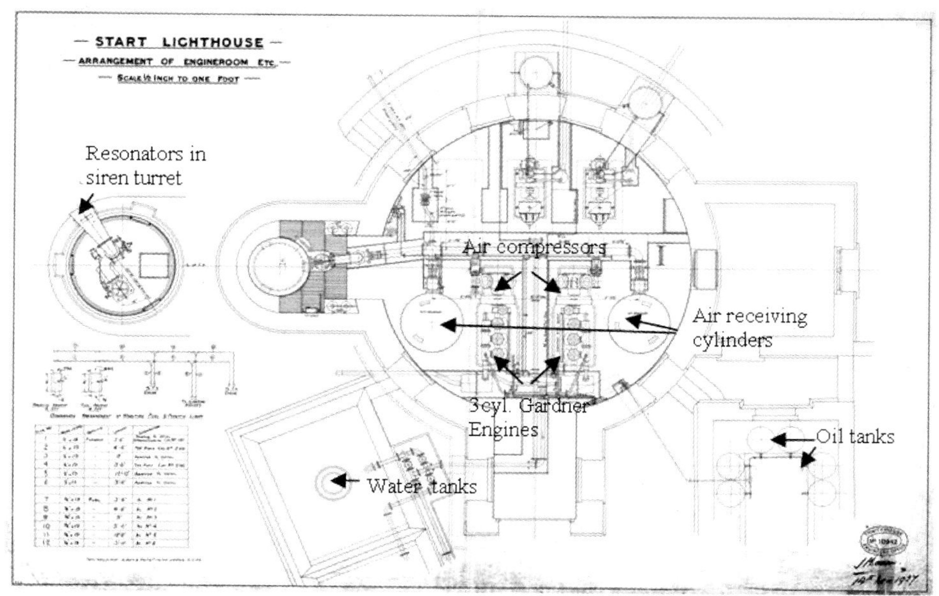

Plan of the 1928 Fog Signal Engine Room. (Trinity House)

8. THE SECOND WORLD WAR

The Threat from the Air

During the Second World War the main threat of attack, particularly after the fall of France, came from the German Luftwaffe. Once again the Start Point lights were extinguished and were only occasionally exhibited on the direction of the naval authorities. Sand bag defences were put in place and in October 1940 the buildings were coated in camouflage paint at a cost of £147. The fog signal continued to be sounded as normal.

Only one report of an air attack on the Lighthouse is recorded in the Station Order Book. The entry for 1 May 1941 states 'no damage was sustained during the recent air raid. The incendiary bombs being quickly extinguished'. In fact the greatest damage suffered during the war was to the approach road and this was caused by friendly forces. One of the many Order Book entries referring to the condition of the road stated that 'heavy vehicles on military duty have again cut up and damaged the approach road'; this was in February 1944, when American forces had largely taken over the area. After one heated exchange with US Army authorities over the demolition of the gate at the top of the approach road, the wartime principal keeper, Tom Abell, was allegedly ordered to exercise greater diplomacy in the interests of preserving the Anglo-American alliance!

Taken after World War II, this photo shows the North Dwelling still disfigured by wartime camouflage. (Judges Ltd)

Most of the military vehicles up at Start would have been connected with the Start Point Radar Station. Even before the outbreak of hostilities, a Chain Home RDS (Radar) station had been established at nearby West Prawle to provide early warning of enemy air raids between Exeter and Plymouth. After the fall of France in 1940, German raids became more frequent, so radar defences were

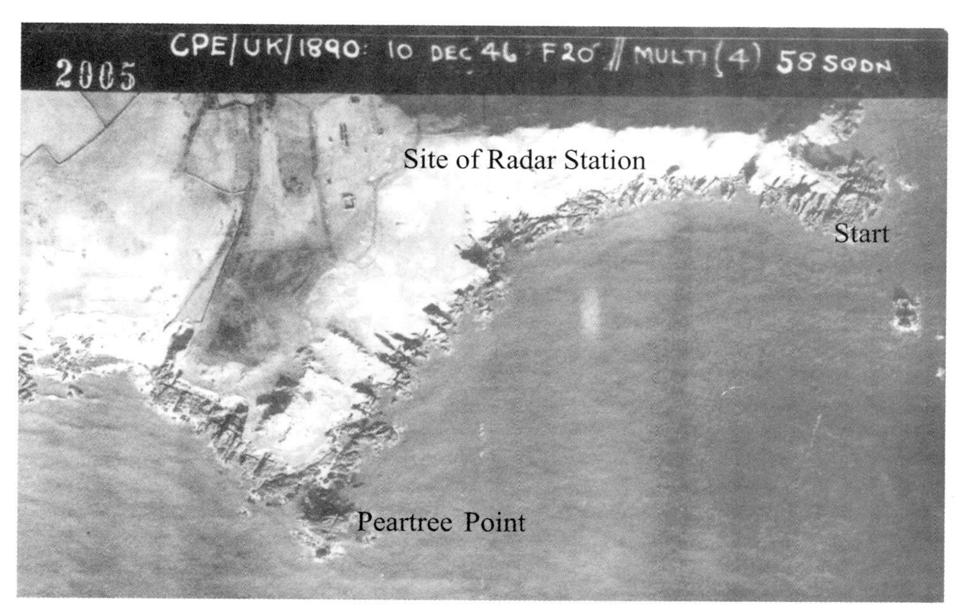

Aerial photo taken in 1946 showing the 'P' shaped compound of the Second World War Radar Station. (Devon County Council)

strengthened with the newly developed Chain Home Low (CHL) system, capable of detecting low-flying enemy aircraft up to twenty-five miles away.[1] Start Point was judged to be a suitable location for CHL and a site on the hill south-east of Start Farm was taken over by the RAF in 1942. On the night of 23/24 April 1943 a Canadian Beaufighter from *RAF Winkleigh* shot down a Junker 88 off the Point—whether it was alerted by the radar is not recorded.

When the Americans moved into the South Hams in 1943, prior to the Normandy Landings, they took over the radar station and re-equipped it with their own Microwave Early Warning radar. The MEW at Start Point (or more precisely Peartree Point) was one of the radars used to plot the progress

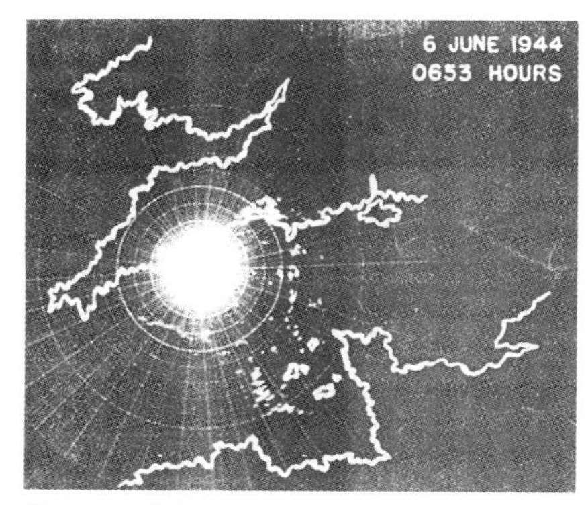

Screen of the American MEW Radar at Start Point showing part of the D-Day invasion on 6 June, 1944. (MIT Museum)

of the D-Day invasion fleet. An aerial photo, taken by the RAF in 1946, shows a single mast standing in the north-east corner of the site near a range of accommodation huts, and a transmitter compound to the south. (The radar mast was erected on almost the same spot as the Admiralty Signal Station had been sited 150 years earlier). The hilltop site was heavily defended with 20mm Oerlikon cannon emplacements, slit trenches and a double-wire perimeter fence. All that can be seen today are the concrete wheel tracks that lead up the hill to a pair of concrete posts.

In addition to radar surveillance, a visual watch was maintained to warn of sea—or airborne attack. On the cliffs overlooking Start Bay and to the east of the BBC Transmitting Station, a Royal Observer Corps observation post was established (near where the Armada Beacon is thought to have been sited 350 years earlier), whilst above the beach at Great Mattiscombe Sand, the Auxiliary Coastguard kept twenty-four hour watch in a lookout hut.

Exercise Tiger

By 1944 the threat of air attack may have receded but the scale of wartime activity on the seas and shores near Start Point intensified. Following the wholesale evacuation of communities from the area to the north of the Lighthouse in November 1943, the Slapton Assault Training Area was established to prepare American troops for the forthcoming D-Day landings on Utah and Omaha Beaches.

Throughout the early months of 1944 the lighthouse keepers and the Observer Corps watch keepers would have looked down on Start Bay and seen countless landing craft and warships taking part in exercises with code-names such as Beaver, Duck and Fox. American troops and equipment would have been seen landing on Slapton Beach to the north, whilst British naval ships maintained a deafening barrage on selected targets and fighters and bombers strafed and bombed positions from the air.

The largest exercise of all, Exercise Tiger, involved troops from the US VII Corps and the 4th Infantry Division and took place between 26th and 29th April. Live ammunition was used throughout the practice assault and it is believed that over 200 hundred men lost their lives as a result of 'friendly fire'.[2] Even greater losses were to take place at sea. On the morning of 27 April 1944, part of Convoy T4, comprising five tank landing ships (LSTs), sailed from Plymouth and around Start Point towards Brixham, escorted by the destroyer *HMS Scimitar* and the corvette *HMS Azalea*.

German E-boats attacking the convoy of LSTs at 2.00am on 22 April 1944, from a painting by E.W. Archer 1995. (Ian Davidson)

The LSTs were large 4500 ton assault vessels, carrying several hundred troops, as well as tanks and lorries. At some point *HMS Scimitar* was rammed by one of the landing craft and forced to return to Plymouth. The convoy, with its remaining escort, was joined off Brixham by three more LSTs and then continued into Lyme Bay.

At about midnight, *HMS Azalea* received a radio message that German E-boats had been spotted in the area. The escort assumed the convoy had received the same message and did not pass it on, but by a cruel twist of fate, the message was not received aboard the LSTs. A typing error in their orders meant that they were on a different frequency. At 2.00am four German E-boats from Cherbourg sank *LST 507* and *LST 531* and badly damaged *LST 289*. The lives of 749 American servicemen were tragically lost. [3]

BBC Transmitting Station, Start Point

Although the part played by Slapton Sands in the preparations for D-Day is well-known, few people are aware that the BBC Transmitting Station at Start Point played an important role in the liberation of Europe, for it was from here that the radio broadcasts for the allied expeditionary forces were transmitted. The BBC Start Point Transmitting Station had been opened just before the outbreak of war, on 14 June 1939, by the Duke of Somerset. The station, at 440ft (134 m) above sea level, had taken two years to build and its function was to transmit the Western Regional Service. Two 450ft (137m) masts provided the aerial system.

The two 450ft (137m) masts at the BBC Start Point Transmitting Station. First erected in 1939, they are still a prominent feature in the landscape today. The original station buildings can be seen on the right. (Cookworthy Museum)

The station was closed when Hitler invaded Poland, but was re-opened in December 1939 for the benefit of the troops in France.[4]

The site was considered vulnerable to ground attack and Nissen huts were built near the entrance gates for troops who patrolled the perimeter fence with dogs. On D-Day plus 2, the station began to transmit the Allied Expeditionary Forces Programme (AEFP), a twenty-four hour service directed at all the armed forces taking part in the landings. British, American and Canadian bands, notably

Glenn Miller's famous forty piece band, played dance music and there was also comedy, war reports and news.

The station also played a part in supporting the French Resistance. Simple codes were devised, such as the repetition of an agreed phrase after a certain interval. Start Point was the only transmitter to broadcast the AEFP from the UK, but later, as the allied advance progressed, relay stations were used to receive the Start Point signal and re-transmit it from mobile transmitters positioned in France and Germany. The service continued until the end of hostilities in Europe.

Between 1945 and 1987 the two transmitters were broadcasting, in turn, the West of England Home Service, Radio 4, Radio 1 and then Radio 2. In 1987 the station was fully automated and the original 1939 buildings replaced by a much smaller unit. When Radio 2 went over to FM, its frequency, 693kHz Medium Wave, was taken over by Radio 5 Live, which is still transmitted from here. In March 1997, all the BBC's domestic transmitting stations were taken over by Castle Transmission International, later to become Crown Castle UK Ltd., and now known as National Grid Wireless.

The BBC Transmitting Station at Start Point. Built in 1939, the imposing building shown here was demolished in 1987. (Cookworthy Museum)

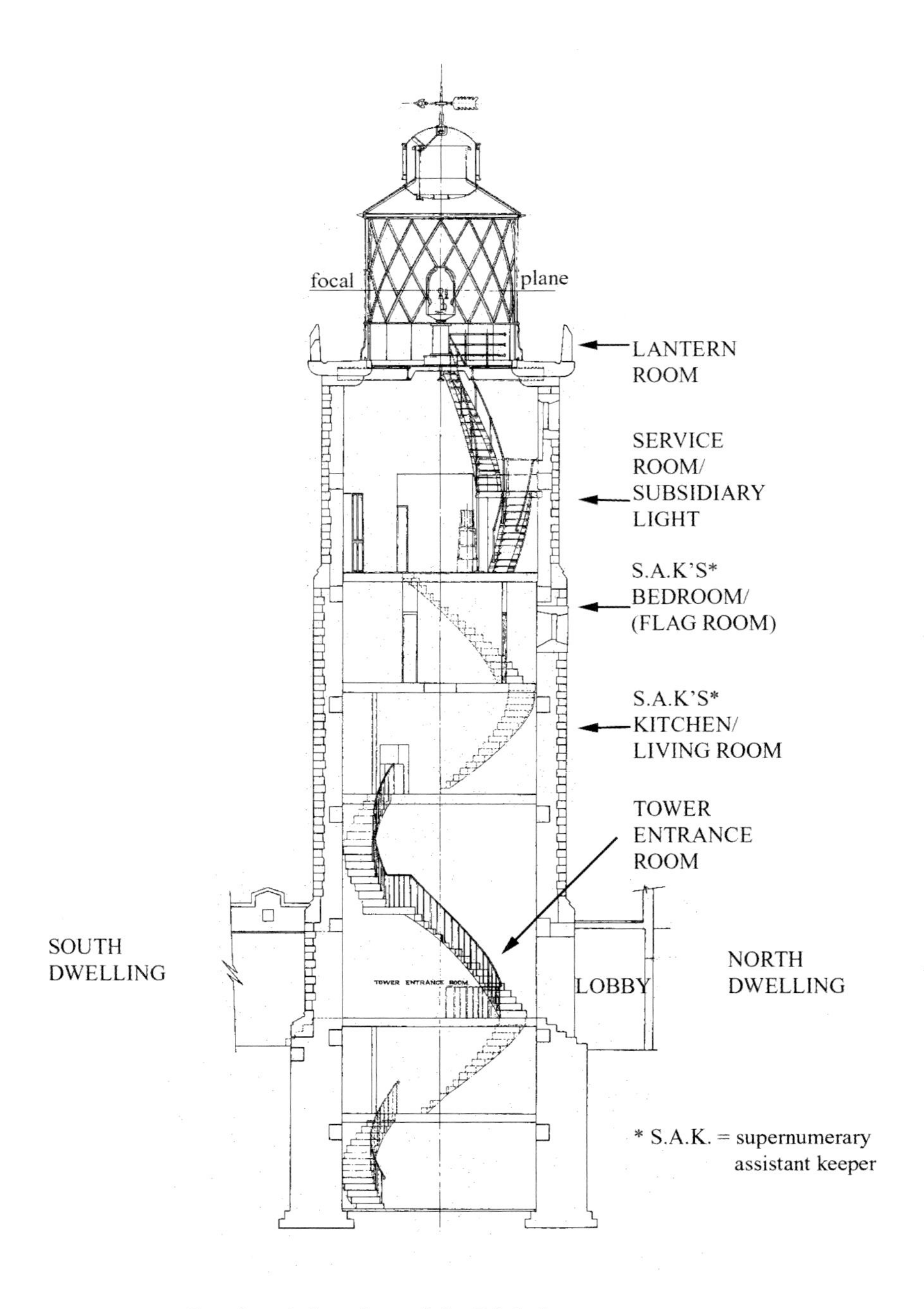

Sectional drawing of the Lighthouse tower.

9. THE LAST KEEPERS

Start Cove. (Claire Pawley)

Lighthouse Electrification 1959

With the War over and the servicemen gone, the keepers' families returned to a way of life largely cut off from the outside world. Apart from the postman with his daily delivery of mail and milk, the only regular visitors were the baker on Mondays, the butcher on Fridays and the grocer once a fortnight in his travelling shop. With their older children boarded out in Kingsbridge during the week, in order to attend secondary school, it could be a lonely existence for the keepers' wives. Their only entertainment, apart from chatting and knitting together in each other's parlour or on the lawn in summer, was listening to the wireless set that ran off re-chargeable accumulators. Interference from the radio beacon meant that even this small pleasure was interrupted every six minutes. The arrival of mains electricity in the late 1950s, however, was to radically change the domestic and working lives of the keepers and their families.

In 1959 the Lighthouse was converted to electrical power and a new light installed over a period of six weeks. The old optic was dismantled and carried in sections down the winding staircase, knocking chips out of the granite stairs in the process. Jim Trout, a former Hallsands fisherman, worked at the Lighthouse during electrification. Forty-seven years on, the old Rayburn range that he helped

Inside the fog signal engine house showing the two sets of Reavell Radial 'Q' type air compressors, each driven by Gardner four-cylinder, diesel engines. One of the two air receiver tanks is on the right. (Association of Lighthouse Keepers)

The Stone Chance 3rd Order optic installed in 1959. (Claire Pawley)

to remove from the kitchen still does good service in his bungalow at Stokenham. Jim also worked on the installation of the new cast-iron and concrete floor in the Lantern Room and helped dismantle the galvanized rainwater collection tank in the Service Room. He vividly recalls the day when a 'runaway' acetylene gas bottle bounced all the way down the spiral stairs and damaged the glazed wooden doors in the ground floor lobby. Needless to say the principal keeper was not happy!

The new electrified light was first lit at sunset on 14 October 1959. It flashed, as it does today, three times every ten seconds. With a diameter of less than 3ft (1m), the new third order Stone Chance optic was only

Going, going... looking down from the top of the Lighthouse it is clear that the leaning Fog Signal Tower is about to collapse, whilst the Engine House, to the right, has already gone. All that remain today are the flat-roofed rectangular building on the left, which contained the water tanks for cooling the diesel engines, and the old Fog Signal Bell-House at the top of the picture. (Association of Lighthouse Keepers)

Lighthouse Automation 1992

Phil Griffiths, the last resident Principal Keeper, 1990-93. (Phil Griffiths)

In August 1992, contractors, LEC Marine, began converting the Lighthouse to full automation at a cost of £82,754. Vast lengths of cabling were installed in order to link all the various controls and mechanisms, via telemetry, to the monitors at the Trinity House Operations Control Centre at Harwich in Essex, 270 miles away. A new halide lamp was placed inside the lens. The Nautophone fog signal, installed in 1983, was dismantled and two of its four emitter units were mounted on the tower parapet. On 27 September 1992, a memorial service was held in the lantern room, by the late Rev. Donald Peyton Jones, to celebrate the 'end of the human hand behind the lighthouse beacon'. Earlier that month, Phil Griffiths, principal keeper since 1990, had handed over the keys to Gordon Partridge, who was to stay on as Keeper-in-Charge, with three assistant keepers. Finally, on 27 January 1993, the last resident keeper left the station. Most of the men transferred to other lighthouses, but their days as resident keepers were numbered. After a ten month spell at Flamborough, Phil Griffiths went to Trevose and then to St Ann's in Pembrokeshire; Gordon Partridge went to the Lizard. All four stations were automated by 1998.

Although fully automated, the Lighthouse remained a working lighthouse requiring regular maintenance, but as Gordon Partridge later observed: 'there was a warmth and a congeniality to a manned lighthouse. After automation we'd visit the lighthouses on maintenance and they were cold and empty and dead. The towers themselves were just the body, the keepers were the heart and soul. Any lighthouse, was only ever as good as its crew. But I loved it there. We had good humour, efficiency and a team that worked really well together'. For men like Phil Griffiths and Gordon Partridge, automation meant the end of an era. Computers had taken over from man.

With the departure of the resident keepers, Peter Kingston, Local Assistant Keeper since 1975 and Keeper-in-Charge from November 1992, started his new role as Attendant. This involved being on call twenty-four hours a day with sole responsibility for maintaining the tower and keeping the light shining.

His first major challenge was to keep the Lighthouse clean whilst the tower was grit-blasted in May 1993. The noise from the grit-blasting was deafening, and it is probably no coincidence that about this time the kittiwakes, nesting on the adjacent cliffs, permanently abandoned their colony. (According to local naturalist Gordon Waterhouse, the new kittiwake colony at nearby Hallsands dates from this time).

Gordon Partridge, the last resident Keeper-in-Charge standing by the controls on the ground floor before automation. (Gordon Partridge)

Peter Kingston, the Attendant Keeper between 1993 and 2000. (P Kingston)

In January 1995, five years after the cliff collapse had sent the engine house into the sea, the Lighthouse was once again under attack by the forces of nature. Peter Kingston was at home after a day's duty. Seconds after he had become aware of a lightning storm over Start Point, he received a call from Operations Control at Harwich to say that all the lighthouse systems were down. Rushing over, he found much of the electrical equipment burnt out and the telephone system blown apart, with thousands of pieces of white insulating plastic scattered like confetti across the ground floor. Lightning had run down a telephone cable to the base of the tower, out along some external cables and had finally run to earth in a disused transformer cable near the wellhouse, causing many thousands of pounds worth of damage in 'a flash'. Trinity House engineers worked day and night to restore normal working.

The Trinity House visiting committee continued to make its annual inspection and the dedication and pride that Peter displayed in his work is clear from the 'glowing' comments made in the Station Order Book by the Deputy Master of Trinity House when he visited in 1994, 1997 and 1999. Peter retired in early 2000 and still lives locally.

The current Attendant, Peter Morgan, is employed by Sir Geoffrey Newman Bt., owner of the Blackpool and Start Estate and provider, under licence, of attendant services. Peter is a former Dartmouth fisherman who knows the waters around Start well. He lives in Stokenham and like Peter Kingston before him, is on twenty-four hour standby.

The tower after grit-blasting in 1993. Note the fog signal emitter stack in the foreground.

10. A VISIT TO THE LIGHTHOUSE

(Tim Stanger)

Enlightening the Public

For seven years, following its automation, the Lighthouse remained closed to the public but in 2000, Sir Geoffrey Newman obtained a licence from Trinity House to provide the attendant services and to conduct public tours. (A year later, the two keepers' cottages, Beacon Cottage, formerly the principal keeper's house, and Landward Cottage, once the North Dwelling, were converted to self-catering holiday accommodation).

The Lighthouse is one of eleven Trinity House lighthouses that welcomes visitors and it is now a significant tourist attraction in the area. The tour appeals to young and old alike and most find it a very enjoyable and 'enlightening' experience. For the spring and summer months at least the lighthouse can no longer be said to be 'cold and empty and dead'.

A Walker's Guide to the Start Point Peninsula

Part of the attraction of a visit to the Lighthouse is the magnificent walk down from the car park at top of the peninsula. Even more spectacular is the longer, and more rugged, footpath walk via Great Mattiscombe and Peartree Point. The

Take your choice! Poole: 168 miles, Minehead: 462 miles, Start Point: ¼ mile. (Author)

two routes, which respectively take about twenty minutes and one hour, can be combined to make one of the finest circular coastal walks on the South Coast.

The routes of this and two other circular walks are shown on the Start Point: Coastal Walks Map at the end of this book (page 86) and are briefly described on page 87. Please note that Start Point and the adjacent coast are included within the Prawle Point and Start Point Site of Special Scientific Interest (SSSI). Walkers are requested to keep to the public footpaths in order to avoid damage to vulnerable habitats.

The car park near Start Farm, is the starting point whichever route is followed. At 330ft (100m) above sea level, it provides a tremendous panorama over the broad sweep of Start Bay, from the ruined village of Hallsands, right round to the Mew Stone and Scabbacombe Head to the east of the entrance to Dartmouth Harbour. On a clear day, it is possible to see the 'Jurassic Coast' of East Devon and Dorset extending as far as Portland Bill to the east. On the other side of the ridge, Lannacombe Bay stretches out to the south. From the car park, the narrow lighthouse road (a public footpath) winds its way down along the gorse and bracken covered northern flanks of the peninsula. In May, a carpet of bluebells presents a magnificent sight. Once past the wooden hut it is worth taking a quick detour onto the footpath which leads up to the top of the ridge. This is also the path to follow for a return to the car park via Peartree Point, after the lighthouse has been visited (Walk 1 on the Coastal Walks map). Those with plenty of stamina could even follow the path to Minehead, which, as the nearby Coast Path sign indicates, is a mere 462 miles away! Poole, at only 168 miles, is 'just up the road'!

From the top of the ridge there is a superb prospect of the sea and the cliffs between Black Stone rocks and Peartree Point. To the left, the spiny crest of the ridge extends, like 'the jagged back of a Stegosaurus' down to the Lighthouse. The rocky outcrops are composed of green schists with quartzite bands. They were first formed as sediments on the sea bed in the Devonian Period, between 345 and 395 million years ago and were later metamorphosed during a mountain building phase in the subsequent Carboniferous Period. A plan of the headland, drawn up by James Walker in 1834, provides the largely forgotten names of the outcrops— names such as Hummock, Prickles, Wrekin, Rough Rocks and Buoy.

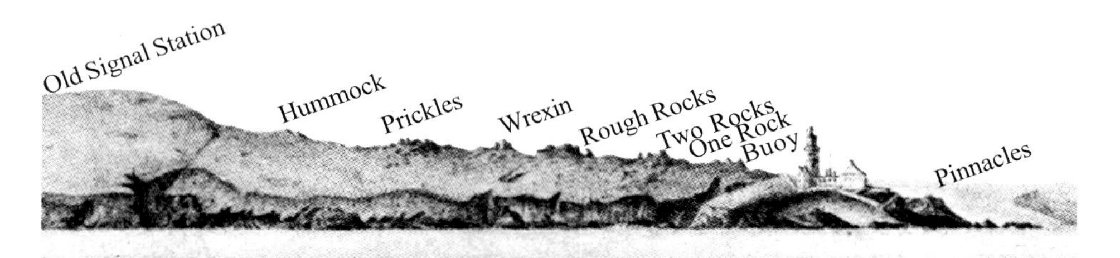

Detail from Admiralty Channel Pilot of 1896. The superimposed names of the rocky outcrops and features on the Peninsula are copied from James Walker's plans. (The Admiralty)

Peregrine falcons can often be seen swooping down from the rocks, whilst closer to hand, stonechats are a common sight, perching on the bracken fronds. A great variety of land and sea birds can in fact be seen on or from, the headland and as Gordon Waterhouse observes in *The Birds and Natural History of the South Hams*, Start Point is an excellent place 'from which to watch land birds migrating overhead. Swallows, larks, pipits and finches follow the line of the coast southwards from Slapton and Hallsands and fly on, over Start to cross the English Channel. When mist or drizzle comes in before dawn, migrants may be

The south facing slope of the rocky promontory. (Author)

gathered in the bracken and tamarisk bushes near the lighthouse. When there are no stars visible for navigation, they are attracted by the lighthouse beams, sometimes fatally, killing themselves against the glass'. [1]

Perhaps the most extreme example of this phenomenon was on the night of 11 May 1861 when, after a severe north-easterly gale, the keeper counted 692 dead birds, mainly skylarks and house sparrows, which together weighed 34lb (15kg).[2] Migrating moths and butterflies are also attracted by the lighthouse beams, including the Hummingbird Hawk-moth from North Africa, for which the Point has become a major landfall.

On the cliffs to the south of the ridge, between Start and Peartree Points, herring and great black-backed gulls, fulmars and shags are a common sight, whilst, on the rocks below, Atlantic grey seals can often be seen at low tide. Returning to the road, the Lighthouse and the neat group of station buildings huddled below it, are soon reached.

A Tour of the Lighthouse

The spiral stairs leading up from the ground floor. (Tim Stanger)

The white-painted lighthouse tower is constructed from blocks of dressed granite.[3] Viewed from the yard the tower rises from its pedestal base in three diminishing stages, with a battlemented parapet projecting out on corbels at the top. Above the parapet, and behind the gallery, is the helical lantern with its thick diamond-shaped glass panes framed in a cast-iron lattice. The lantern has a diameter of 14ft (4.2m) whilst the glazing has a clear height of 10ft (3m). The lantern is roofed with a domed copper canopy which is surmounted by a weathervane. The tower is pierced by a number of small windows, some of which are roundheaded; all have plain raised surrounds. The door in the main entrance porch has a Tudor arch, above which the raised parapet bears the Trinity House

The lower basement with the central cast-iron trunk for the clockwork weight and the slate benches for the oil tanks. (Tim Stanger)

The standby Lister generator in the upper basement. (Tim Stanger)

arms, with the motto 'Trinitas in Unitate' ('Three in One').

The **ground floor** room of the tower rises to a considerable height. The most notable feature is the cantilevered granite staircase and its iron balustrade which spirals up to the floor above. Before 1872 the ground floor was the keeper's parlour and there was an additional floor of living accommodation just above, at the level of the small landing. In the centre of the high ceiling there was a circular aperture through which, until 1959, the 5cwt (250kg) lead weights, that set the revolving optic in motion, fell, like the weights of a giant grandfather clock, through a trunk or tube right down to the base of the tower. Opposite the entrance and behind a pair of glazed doors, a short flight of steps lead down to what was the South Dwelling entrance lobby.

There are two **basement** levels. The lower level was originally used as an oil store where hundred gallon oil tanks were mounted on slate benches. From these tanks the keepers filled their five gallon drums and then carried them up to the lamp above. The room has also been used as a coal store. The upper basement was originally a kitchen, and later a workshop and store. After the fog signal engine house was abandoned, a 12.5kVA standby generator, powered by a Lister TS3 diesel engine, was installed here in 1985. Should the mains supply fail, the generator will start up

The circular kitchen. (Tim Stanger)

automatically and power the whole station. Back on the **ground floor** the visitor would have seen, in the days between electrification in 1959 and automation in 1993, an array of instruments around the walls, telling the keeper at a glance of any faults. Telemetry cabling and equipment now line the walls. One of the grey boxes, the Telemetry Control Cubicle, sends regular status reports on all the lighthouse systems, as well as alarms when faults arise, to the Operations Control Centre at Harwich via a BT telephone cable, and receives control signals from Harwich back down the same line.

Up the spiralling steps, the first floor held the **supernumeraries' kitchen and living room**. The main feature in this room, before electrification in 1959, was a cast-iron, coal-fired range. Above, the room now called the **Flag Room** was, prior to automation, a bedroom for the supernumerary assistant keepers. In this small space were three ordinary beds (not the curved 'banana beds' used on rock lighthouses), wardrobes and bedside cabinets. The flag locker, with its complete set of International Code of Signal flags, was previously in the entrance lobby of the tower. The wooden frame holding the diamond and half-diamond shaped, spare glazing for the lantern was kept in the under-stairs cupboard. Also on display are the PK's telescope and a standard five gallon brass and copper oil can.

The Flag Room, with International Code Signal flags, the Keeper's Telescope and a five gallon oil drum. (Tim Stanger)

Next on the way up is the **Service room** which houses the red sector subsidiary light for the Skerries Bank. Here the red-shaded prisms project a fixed beam, within a 45° horizontal arc, over twelve miles. The light has a 500 watt, 100 volt lamp. Behind it is the back-up: a tiny 100 watt, 12 volt lamp.

In 1992 a modest grey box in this room, the Navigation Lights Control Cubicle which monitors the lights, effectively replaced the resident keepers. Previously, the duty keeper, in between keeping an eye on the lights and looking out to sea, would have sat at a desk in this room and filled in the weather log every three hours. Before 1872 there was an additional floor between the present Service room and the Lantern above. The Skerries fixed light, and the clockwork machinery for the revolving light above, were originally installed on this floor.

The small red sector light in front of the metal stairs leading to the lantern room. (Tim Stanger)

Two steep metal stairs lead up to the **Lantern room,** where the main light is magnified through the revolving optic (see photograph on page 85). The smell and heat of the oil lamp and the sound of its clockwork drive once filled this space, but today the optic quietly rotates around a 1000 watt, 240 volt electric lamp. Should this lamp fail, an automatic switch rotates a lamp changer which brings into focus a second 1000 watt lamp. If the power supply fails, both lamps can operate off the generator until normal service is resumed. Should that fail, a bank of 24volt batteries can provide power for seventy-two hours. Further back-up is provided by an Emergency Lantern fitted with a twin filament 60 watt lamp, and a flasher unit. This is mounted on top of the optic and has a range of ten nautical miles.

The revolving optic, manufactured by Stone Chance and installed in 1959, is a small third order catadioptric. *Third order* is a measure of the optic's size in terms of focal length—the distance from the light source to the lens. The focal length of a small third order is 375mm. A *catadioptric* system is similar to the dioptric optic described on page 18, but it has reflecting, as well as refracting prisms, to focus all the light into a single beam.

The optic has six panels of lenses (in two groups of three) mounted in a gun-metal frame. When the optic revolves around the light source, it produces a beam of three white flashes every ten seconds over a range of twenty-five sea miles

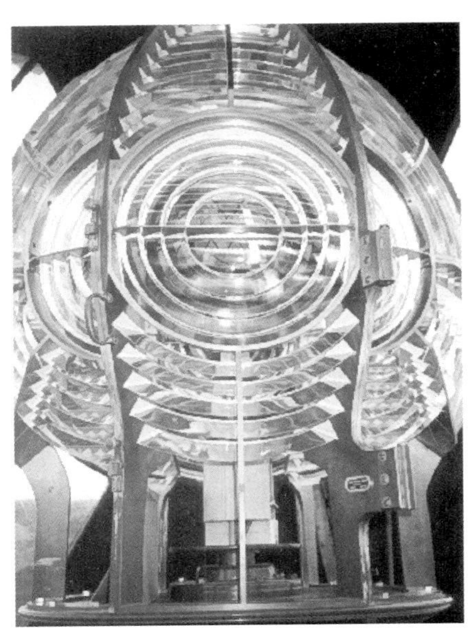

The revolving optic, showing on the left, one of the two panels of three bull's eye lenses which focus the light to give three flashes in succession. On the right is the intervening eclipse phase. (Gordon Partridge)

(46km). The flashes, each lasting 0.3 of a second, are packaged between two eclipses lasting 1.3 seconds and a third eclipse lasting 6.5 seconds. This instantly recognisable 'character' provides a ready 'fix' for mariners.

The optic is mounted on a Stone Chance pedestal, the turntable of which revolves clockwise, by means of an electrical drive, once every twenty seconds. A second electrical drive provides back-up, but should this fail the optic can be cranked round by hand.

When the Lighthouse was manned, the revolving optic was curtained off by day to keep the sun off the lens, otherwise the focused rays of the sun would have caused serious damage to the equipment inside the lantern. Today, with no keepers to pull the curtains, it is necessary to keep the optic rotating at all times.

The outside gallery of the lantern is accessed by a small low door with a 'monkey fist' grasping the door handle—a standard Trinity House detail. One of the most hazardous of the keepers' tasks, particularly in bad weather, was keeping the outside of the lantern windows clean. A ladder, attached to a runner around the top of the lantern, was used to reach the top panes. Mounted on the castellated

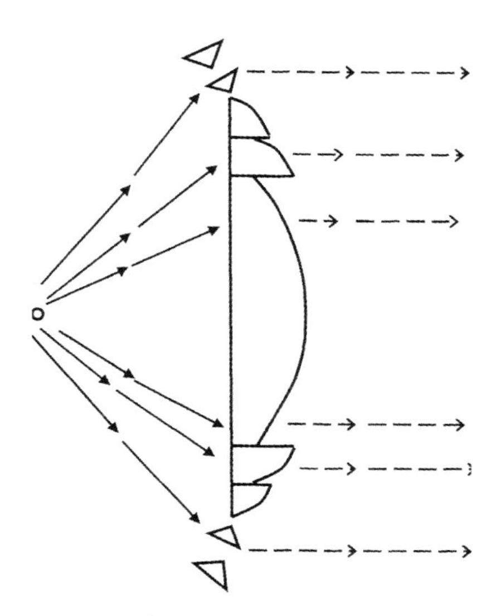

The catadioptric system uses a Fresnel lens (centre) to refract light, in combination with rings of reflecting prisms (top and bottom). (Lynn Pearson/ Shire Publications)

The 'monkey fist' handle on the lantern gallery door—a standard Trinity House detail. (Claire Pawley)

parapet of the gallery, the Fog Detector, a VF-500 forward-scatter visibility sensor, constantly monitors the atmosphere and activates the nearby Fog Signal Emitter, whenever visibility is reduced to under two miles. The detector works on the principle that particles of water, suspended in foggy air, scatter light. One arm transmits a beam of light and the receiver, in the other arm, measures the amount of light that is scattered in a sample volume of air. The electrically powered Fog Signal Emitter stack comprises two 500Hz ELU-500 emitter units which sound a 138 decibel, three second blast every minute. The sound is produced by a steel membrane, suspended between the pole sections of a magnet, which vibrates when the current is switched on. In daytime, if the foghorn goes off, the light also comes on.

The parapet was the only means of escape in the event of a fire in the tower below. In the early days a knotted rope, or at best a rope ladder, would be suspended from the parapet and supernumerary keepers, as part of their training, had to prove that they had the courage to 'go over the top'. Nowadays the escape equipment box in the lantern room contains a Davy harness that automatically lowers an evacuee at 3ft (1m) per second.

The electric Fog Signal Emitter stack mounted on the parapet. (Author)

Peter Kingston pointing to the Fog Detector, also mounted on the parapet. (Peter Kingston)

Looking to the Future

A key part of the Lighthouse's attraction for visitors is that, in spite of automation, it remains a working lighthouse. But, with the rapid development of satellite navigation systems and sophisticated terrestrial radio-navigation systems, the future of the traditional lighthouse, as something more than just a museum, is clearly uncertain. The building itself is protected, having been listed as a building of historical and architectural interest in 1967 (the piggeries and well-house were listed in 1990), but for how much longer will its guiding light continue to shine?

In October 2004, Trinity House, together with the lighthouse authorities of Scotland and Ireland, the General Lighthouse Authorities (GLAs), published VISION 2020,[4] a review of the future of marine aids to navigation over the next fifteen years. They concluded that, although lighthouses will continue to play an important role in providing back-up for satellite navigation, sectors to mark dangers and leading lights for safe channel approaches, their use for landfall and waypoint navigation will continue to decline.

The GLAs subsequently published, in 2005, a Joint Review of Aids to Navigation which recommended the discontinuance of ten lighthouses.[5] The review revealed that some 13,380 commercial vessel movements take place annually within a twenty mile radius of Start Point Lighthouse—well within the range of its main light. A survey of all categories of mariner, carried out as part of the review, confirmed that the Start Light is highly valued as an aid to navigation and so the Lighthouse is not under any immediate threat.

Start Point Lighthouse has been shining its guiding light for mariners for one hundred and seventy years. Those who appreciate its special qualities, on both land and sea, will earnestly hope that it continues to do so. With apologies to Henry Longfellow*, may it:

**adapted from 'The Lighthouse' by Henry Wadsworth Longfellow. (Trinity House)*

REFERENCES

Key unpublished sources relating to the history and development of the Lighthouse are *Start Point Station Order Book*, 1850 to the present; *Trinity House Board Minutes* (Ms 30010), and the *Warden's Committee Minutes* (Ms 30025) in the Guildhall Library, London.

Chapter 1. The Sea be Fair Wicked 'ere

1. Kennerley, Alston. *New Maritime History of Devon, Vol. II, Shiphandling and Hazards on the Devon Coast,* Conway Maritime Press, London, 1994.
2. Fuller, Thomas. *Worthies of England,* 1652.
3. Cattell, Raymond. *Under Sail Through Red Devon,* A. Maclehouse, 1937

Chapter 2. Early History

1. *Chanter 13, The Register of Bishop Oldham, folio 139,* Devon Record Office (DRO).
2. *Chanter 15, The Register of Bishop Veysey, folio 84,* DRO.
3. Polwhele, Richard. *History of Devonshire,* 1793, reproduced by Kohler and Coombe, Dorking, 1977
4. Russell, Percy. *Fire Beacons in Devon,* Transactions of the Devonshire Assoc., 1955.
5. Elliot, Colin. *Discovering Armada Britain,* David & Charles, Newton Abbot, 1987.
6. Hanson, Neil. *The Confident Hope of a Miracle, the True Story of the Spanish Armada,* Corgi Books, London, 2003.
7. Finsberg, HPR *The Customs of Stokenham,* in *West Country Historical Studies,* David & Charles, Newton Abbot, 1969.
8. Waterhouse, Robert. *Stokenham Heritage Appraisal,* South Hams District Council, Totnes, 2002.
9. Wilkinson D. & Boyle M. *Lighthouses, A Photographic Memory,* Francis Frith, Salisbury, 2001.
10. Waugh, Mary. *Smuggling in Devon & Cornwall 1700-1850,* Countryside Books, Newbury, 1991.

Chapter 3. The Threat from France

1. Kitchen, Frank. *The Napoleonic War Signal Stations,* Mariners' Mirror, Vol. LXXVI, pp337-344, 1990.
2. Wilson, Geoffrey. *The Old Telegraphs,* Phillimore, Chichester, 1976.
3. Cordingly, David. *Billy Ruffian,* Bloomsbury, London, 2003.

Chapter 4. Building the Lighthouse

1. Oppenheim, M.M., *The Maritime History of Devon,* Univ. of Exeter, 1968.
2. Smith, Dennis. *James Walker (1781-1862): Civil Engineer,* Newcomen Society, 2004.
3. Chrimes, M.M. *Hugh McIntosh (1768-1840), National Contractor,* Newcomen Society, 2004.
4. Fox, Sarah Prideaux. *Kingsbridge Estuary & Rambles in the Neighbourhood,* Kingsbridge, 1864.
5. Wilkinson D. & Boyle M., *Lighthouses, A Photographic Memory,* Francis Frith, Salisbury, 2004.

Chapter 5. The Victorian and Edwardian Lighthouse 1864-1912

1. Fox, S.P. 1864, *op. cit.*
2. White, Walter, quoted in *Our Lighthouses and Lightships,* WH Davenport Adams, Nelson, London 1891.
3. Fairweather, James, *Salcombe & Neighbourhood,* Salcombe, 1884.
4. Fairweather, James, *op. cit.*
5. Milton, R. & F. *Sisters Against the Sea,* Halsgrove, Tiverton, 2005.
6. Bathurst, Bella. *The Lighthouse Stevensons,* Harper Collins, London, 1999.

Chapter 6. For Those In Peril on the Sea

1. Fairweather, James. *Eyewitness Accounts of the Great Blizzard, March 1891.* Kingsbridge History Society, Kingsbrige, 2002.
2. Alexander, Henry G.L. *The Life & Death of the Liverpool Barque Dryad (1874-91),* Aunemouth Books, Kingsbridge, 2004.

Chapter 7. The Great War and its Aftermath

1. Trinity House Stores, Penzance. *Letter to Principal Keeper,* 4th April 1913. Association of Lighthouse Keepers.
2. Belloc, Hilaire. *The Cruise of the Nona,* Constable, London, 1925.
3. Larn, Richard. *Shipwrecks of the South Devon Coast,* Countryside Books, Newbury, 1996.
4. McDonald, Kendall. *Dive South Devon,* Underwater World, Teddington, 1995.
5. Murch, D. & Fairweather, L. *Wreck and Rescue on the South Hams Coast,* Salcombe, 1980.
6. Milton, R. & F., *op. cit.*
7. Wasley, Gerald. *Devon in the Great War,* Devon Books, Tiverton, 2000.

Chapter 8. The Second World War

1. Latham, C. & Stobbs, A., *Radar, the Wartime Miracle,* Sutton Publishing, Stroud, 1996.
2. Small, Ken. *The Forgotten Dead,* Bloomsbury, London, 1998.
3. Rose-Price, Robin & Parnell, Jean. *The Land We Left Behind,* Orchard Publications, Chudleigh, Devon, 2004.
4. Frost, Stuart. *Brief History of Start Point Transmitting Station*, author, 1984.

Chapter 9. The Last Keepers

1. *Evening Herald,* 14 February, 1990.

Chapter 10. A Visit to the Lighthouse

1. Waterhouse, Gordon. *The Birds and Natural History of the South Hams,* Orchard Publications, Chudleigh, Devon, 2000.
2. Fairweather, James. *Salcombe & Neighbourhood,* 1884.
3. Dept. of the Environment. *List of Buidings of Architectural or Historic Interest.*
4. The General Lighthouse Authorities. *Vision 2020,* London, 2004.
5. The General Lighthouse Authorities. *Aids to Navigation Review,* 2005

RECOMMENDED FURTHER READING

Lighthouses

Lighthouses of Trinity House, Thomas Reed Publications, Bradford-on-Avon, 2002.

Lighthouses, Lynn F. Pearson, Shire Publications, Princes Risborough, 2003.

Lighthouses, to Light Their Way, Martin Boyle, B&T Publications, Southampton, 1996.

Lighthouses, Towers of the Sea, Payton, C. et al, The National Trust, London, 2005.

Spanish Armada

The Confident Hope of a Miracle, Neil Hutton, Corgi Books, London, 2003.

Napoleon & the Bellerophon

Billy Ruffian, David Cordingly, Bloomsbury, London, 2003.

Wrecks

Shipwrecks of the South Hams, Kendall McDonald, Wreckwalker Books, Kingsbridge, 2002

Shipwrecks of the Devon Coast, Richard Larn, Countryside Books, Newbury, 1996.

The Great Blizzard 1891, Kingsbridge History Society Reprint, Kingsbridge, 2002.

The Life & Death of the Liverpool Barque Dryad, (1874-91), Henry G.L. Alexander, Aunemouth Books, Kingsbridge, 2004.

Hallsands History

Sisters Against the Sea, Milton, R. & F. , Halsgrove, Tiverton, 2005.

Hallsands, A Village Betrayed, Steve Melia, Forest Publishing, Newton Abbot, 2002

World War II, Exercise Tiger

The Forgotten Dead, Ken Small, Bloomsbury, London, 1998.

The Land We Left Behind, Robin Rose-Price & Jean Parnell, Orchard Publications, Chudleigh, Devon, 2004.

The Invasion Before Normandy, Edwin P. Hoyt, Robert Hale, London, 1987

Wildlife

Wildlife Walks in the South Hams, Gordon Waterhouse, Orchard Publications, Chudleigh, Devon, 2004.

The Birds and Natural History of the South Hams, Gordon Waterhouse, Orchard Publications, Chudleigh, Devon, 2000.

Geology

Classic Landforms of the South Devon Coast, Derek Mottershead, Geographical Association, Sheffield, 1997.

Websites

www.trinityhouse.co.uk.	Trinity House.
www.alk.org.uk	Association of Lighthouse Keepers.

VISITING THE LIGHTHOUSE

For details of visiting times phone 01803 770606 or visit the website: www.trinityhouse.co.uk

The Lighthouse is signposted off the A379, between Dartmouth and Kingsbridge, at the Carehouse Cross roundabout, Stokenham, South Devon.

Safety Notice: visitors who wish to climb the stairs to the top of the Lighthouse, must be over one metre in height. Anyone suffering from vertigo, heart or respiratory conditions, is advised not to undertake the tour.

STAYING IN THE LIGHTHOUSE COTTAGES

Two cottages are available: Beacon Cottage (sleeps 6) and Landward Cottage (sleeps 5).

Details can be obtained from Trinity House. Phone 020 7481 6900.

Website: www.trinityhouse.co.uk.

Start Point from Torcross. (Author)

The revolving optic in the centre of the lantern room. (Tim Stanger)

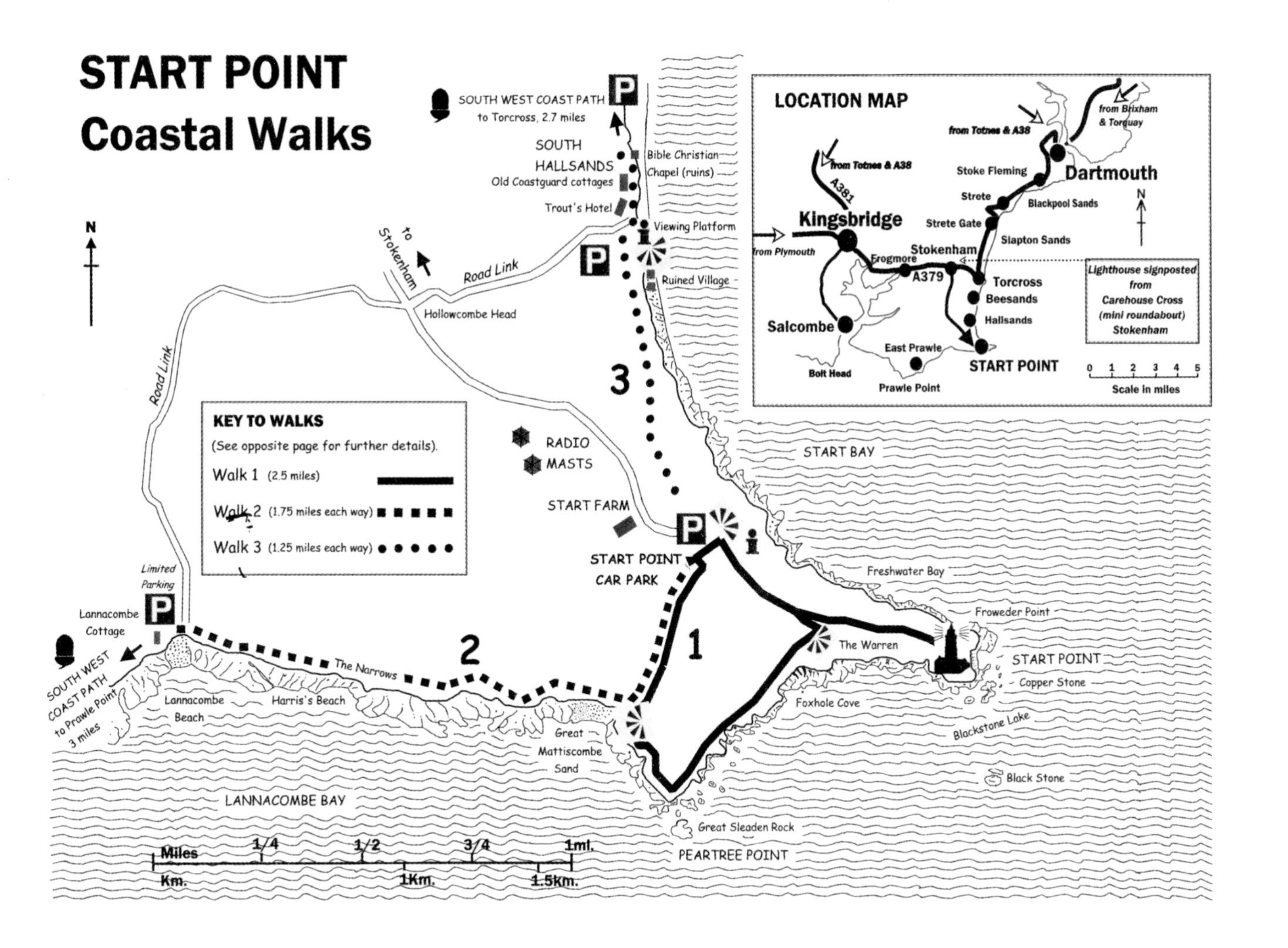
START POINT
Coastal Walks
SOUTH WEST COAST PATH
to Torcross, 2.7 miles
SOUTH
HALLSANDS
Old Coastguard cottages
Trout's Hotel
Bible Christian
Chapel (ruins)
Viewing Platform
Ruined Village
to
Stokenham
Road Link
Hollowcombe Head
Road Link
N
KEY TO WALKS
(See opposite page for further details).
Walk 1 (2.5 miles)
Walk 2 (1.75 miles each way)
Walk 3 (1.25 miles each way)
RADIO
MASTS
START FARM
START POINT
CAR PARK
START BAY
Freshwater Bay
Froweder Point
The Warren
START POINT
Copper Stone
Foxhole Cove
Blackstone Lake
Black Stone
Great Sleaden Rock
PEARTREE POINT
Limited
Parking
Lannacombe
Cottage
SOUTH WEST
COAST PATH
to Prawle Point
3 miles
Lannacombe
Beach
Harris's Beach
The Narrows
Great
Mattiscombe
Sand
LANNACOMBE BAY
1
2
3
Miles
1/4
1/2
3/4
1ml.
Km.
1Km.
1.5km.
LOCATION MAP
from Totnes & A38
from Brixham
& Torquay
from Totnes & A38
A381
Kingsbridge
from Plymouth
Frogmore
Stokenham
A379
Stoke Fleming
Dartmouth
Strete
Blackpool Sands
Strete Gate
Slapton Sands
Torcross
Beesands
Hallsands
Salcombe
East Prawle
START POINT
Bolt Head
Prawle Point
N
Lighthouse signposted
from
Carehouse Cross
(mini roundabout)
Stokenham
0 1 2 3 4 5
Scale in miles

START POINT: A GUIDE TO COASTAL WALKS

The three walks shown on the map are all on public footpaths and all start from the car park at Start Point. Walks 2 and 3 are linear but can be linked to form a circular walk by following the narrow roads via Hollowcombe Head (total distance: 4.75 miles), or via Kellaton and Bickerton to the north (total distance: 6 miles). The Ordnance Survey map for the area is the Explorer OL20, South Devon.

Walk 1. A circular walk around the Start Point peninsula via the Lighthouse, Peartree Point and Great Mattiscombe Sand, giving spectacular views across Start Bay to the north and Lannacombe Bay to the south. Part of the walk follows the narrow approach road to the Lighthouse but the remainder is on rough paths. Care is needed on the rocky section below the cliffs near Peartree Point. A description of the wildlife and scenery to be seen on this walk is given on pages 69 to 72.

Walk 2. A coast path walk to Lannacombe Beach via Great Mattiscombe Sands, both of which are beautiful sandy beaches with superb views across Lannacombe Bay. The first section of the walk down from the car park to Great Mattiscombe can be rough and muddy in places, but the coast path itself provides easy walking along the terrace of fields that lie between the coastal slope above and the rocky raised beaches below. There is limited parking for about twelve cars above Lannacombe Beach (privately owned/fee payable). The walk can be extended along the coast path to East Prawle village (2 miles from Lannacombe Beach) where there are two pubs (Pig's Nose and Providence Inn), a shop and café, public toilets, parking, B&B and camping; or, a little further on, to Prawle Point where there is a National Trust car park (3 miles from Lannacombe Beach).

Walk 3. Another coast path walk, this time dropping down to Hallsands, with impressive views across the wide sweep of Start Bay. South Hallsands is well worth visiting, particularly when Trout's Hotel is open and serving cream teas! Just below the hotel is a path leading to a viewing platform overlooking the ruined fishing village. Display panels tell the story of the events leading up to the destruction of the village in 1917. Beyond Trout's Hotel are the former coastguard cottages and the ruined Bible Christian Chapel perched above the cliffs (now the home of a kittiwake colony). Parking is available in the privately owned car park 100 metres to the west of Trout's Hotel (free parking for visitors to Trout's Servery and the ruined village). The walk can be extended to the beach at North Hallsands (0.3 miles from South Hallsands - free car parking); on to Beesands village and the Cricket Inn (1.5 miles from South Hallsands - public toilets, free car parking, B&B, camping), and beyond that to Torcross (2.5 miles from South Hallsands) with its pubs (Torcross Tavern and Start Bay Inn), cafés, gift shops and post office, public toilets, car parking (fee payable) and B&B.

PLEASE KEEP DOGS AND CHILDREN UNDER CLOSE SUPERVISION AND RESPECT THE COUNTRY CODE